"If you don't
love something,
then don't
do it."

D1151702

THE **POWER**
OF DOING
LESS

Fergus O'Connell

CAPSTONE
A Wiley Brand

Registered office
Capstone Publishing Ltd. (A Wiley Company), John Wiley and Sons Ltd, The Atrium, Southern Gate, Chichester, West Sussex, PO19 8SQ, United Kingdom

For details of our global editorial offices, for customer services and for information about how to apply for permission to reuse the copyright material in this book please see our website at www.wiley.com.

Library of Congress Cataloging-in-Publication Data is available

A catalogue record for this book is available from the British Library.

ISBN 978-0-857-08421-7 (paperback)
ISBN 978-0-857-08419-4 (ebk)   ISBN 978-0-857-08418-7 (ebk)

Cover design: Mackerel Ltd

Set in 11/13 pt FuturaStd by Toppan Best-set Premedia Limited

Printed in Great Britain by TJ International Ltd, Padstow, Cornwall, UK

For Mandy and Eamonn

Contents

TO THE HESITATING PURCHASER viii

OVERLOADED? I'LL BET YOU ARE x

MAYBE IT'S TIME FOR A CHANGE xiv

1 THIS PROBLEM IS REALLY SERIOUS 1

2 WHY TIME MANAGEMENT COURSES DON'T WORK 13

3 YOU WILL NEVER GET EVERYTHING DONE 25

4 KNOWING WHAT THE "RIGHT STUFF" IS 41

5 FILTER ONE: TO DO OR NOT TO DO 63

6 FILTER TWO: DOING IT ON YOUR TERMS 89

7 DON'T FEEL GUILTY 105

8 IT'S ABOUT GOOD HABITS 121

9 THE HARVEST 133

"The one charm of the past
is that it is the past."

- OSCAR WILDE, *The Picture of Dorian Gray*

To The Hesitating Purchaser

Chances are that at least ten months will have passed between the sunny morning I am writing these words and the day you get to read them. How will those ten months have been for you? Will they have been packed full of doing the things that really matter to you, progressing various projects, spending time with people you love to spend time with, enjoying life and all the richness it has to offer?

Or will the last ten months have been a weary succession of unremarkable or frantically busy or less-than-life-enhancing days?

Either way, it doesn't matter that much. They're gone. Those ten months, three hundred or so days, ain't coming round again. You've seen the last of them. *They* won't be back.

But the next ten months haven't come. Tomorrow hasn't happened yet. If you're not happy with the way the last ten months have been, that doesn't mean that the next ten have to be like that. You can change them. A little or a lot, depending on how close or how far away they were from your ideal.

And to do this, you don't have to do *more*.

In fact, you don't have to do much at all.

Actually – and this is the really nice thing – you have to do a lot less.

Sound good? Better head for the checkout.

"It is nothing to die.
It is frightful not to live."

- VICTOR HUGO, *Les Misérables*

Overloaded? I'll Bet You Are

Have you ever stopped to figure out how much you have to do versus how much time you have to do it? Probably not. Probably too scary!

In an ideal world, you'd presumably love to have more time available for new or unexpected things. Have time to just "be", catch a breath and think about your job and your life. Maybe be creative, find new or better ways of doing things, get ideas, inspiration even.

But the likelihood is that you're overloaded. There's an exercise I do on the courses I teach where I get people to figure out how much work they have to do versus how much time they have available to do it. Back in the 1990s, overload levels of 30 to 50% were pretty common – with the occasional person being a 100% or more overloaded.

Nowadays, I find that at least half the people I do this exercise with *are a 100% or more overloaded*. Let's be clear what this means.

That's twice as much work as they have time available to do. Overload levels of 200% are not uncommon. I have seen people more than 300% overloaded.

Of course, this just confirms what we all already know. We are becoming even busier – not only in work but in life generally. As each year goes by, we find ourselves working harder and harder. We spend more time at work, thinking about work, bringing work home with us. Work now invades our personal life in a way that would have been unimaginable only a few years ago or to our parents. And as a result of this invasion of and consequent reduction in our personal time, we find we are now madly busy outside of work as well.

Remember when the media used to talk about having to "educate people for leisure"? The very notion raises a bitter or incredulous laugh these days.

And the stress related to all of this has increased. As I write this we are about four years into what will probably become known as the Second Great Depression. There is no real sign that it is going to end any time soon. And so there are layoffs, redundancies, downsizing, offshoring.

"You're lucky to have a job."

"You'll have to do more with less."

"Just work smarter not harder" (whatever that's supposed to mean).

"If you don't do it we'll find somebody who will."

"We have no choice, we have to do it."

Any of this sound familiar?

It's this . . .

. . . when it really should be – this.

So, how are we to deal with all this? How are we to continue to take on these massive levels of work? And even if we can climb to the top of this work mountain, what about the rest of our lives? Our loved ones, families, children, hopes, dreams, ambitions, things we wanted to do with our lives that have nothing to do with work or earning a living? Is life in the industrial world in the 21st century just to be about work, bringing home the bacon and paying the mortgage?

And of course the answer is that it had better not be. Our lives had better not end up like that. And they don't have to.

Because there is a way out of all of this.

And to find the way, all you have to do is learn one simple skill.

You have to learn to do less.

"They always say time changes things, but you actually have to change them yourself."

- ANDY WARHOL

Maybe It's Time For a Change

All books have a "promise". The promise of *The Power Of Doing Less* is pretty straightforward. If you read this book *and do the things that it says*, then:

- If you are a person who finds themselves stressed all the time with too much to do and never enough time to do it, then that situation will change dramatically for the better.
- If you are a person who leaves work late and feeling guilty because so many things still haven't been done (or, in fact, you're feeling guilty just because you're leaving), then you will find yourself getting out on time and not feeling any guilt whatsoever.
- If you find there are "never enough hours in the day", you will find great swathes of time opening up for you.
- If you feel that life is passing you by and you are not getting to do the things you really want to do, then you will find a new focus on those things and not only that, but time available to do them.
- If you are the sort of person who takes on endless new projects eagerly because they excite you, and then subsequently feel irritated because you don't have time to finish them as comprehensively as you'd like, then you'll find time opening up and becoming available so that you can complete these things properly.

- If you are a person whose instinctive reaction, when somebody asks you to do something, is "How can I fit this in to an already overcrowded life?" you will become a person who asks, "Why should I invest my precious time in this?"

Just think about this for a few moments. *Feel* what that would be like. A new you at work, doing an outstanding job and still having a life. That life full of the richness that you've always wanted – the people, the ambitions and hopes and dreams that you have. Less stress – a feeling that you are controlling your time rather than being a slave to or victim of it.

> You will find great swathes of time opening up for you.

You'd have more personal time – the rare and precious "me" time. You'd spend more time with the people that you love – children, husbands, wives, partners, loved ones. You'd get to be more creative in the things you do already – notably your job. You'd have time to draw breath and think about what you do and ways you might do it better. You'd have more time to collaborate because you wouldn't be spending all your time just trying to keep your own head above water.

And then of course, there are all the new things you could do or take up. Get fit or get in shape again – if that's something you've let fall by the wayside. Learn a new skill – a foreign language, for instance, or a musical instrument or a new hobby. Or explore that long-held business idea that you've had. You could travel, if that was your thing. There's so much you could do with this time.

And you know, you might end up actually prolonging your life. Your stress levels would have gone way down and if you were taking care of your body again, then who knows what the knock-on effects of that could be?

All sounds pretty good, huh?

Of course, the key thing is that you've got to do what the book says. It isn't enough just to read it. That'd be some book, wouldn't it – if all you had to do was read it and these changes would magically occur in your life? No, the book isn't quite that good. But it's probably the next best thing. You don't have to do more things to make the book work for you. *In fact, you have to do less.*

I teach an online course in *The Power Of Doing Less* and recently, somebody was trying to make up their mind about whether or not to join the course. They asked me if I could give them "an estimate of the time that a delegate would spend doing the exercises and tests"?

My reply began like this: "I don't mean this to sound weird, but the exercises mainly involve *not* doing things. Turning things down, declining things, basically working out what doesn't need doing and focusing only on the things that really bring value."

The Power Of Doing Less sets out to teach you a new skill and in the process, to change your behaviour. The skill is not complicated or difficult to understand – indeed, it's blindingly simple. It's not difficult to learn. But changing your behaviour is difficult – no question of that. And causing people to change their behaviour by stuff you've written in a book isn't exactly a walk in the park either.

The key to this behaviour change is to try the little challenges that I give you to do in each chapter. When you get asked to do something, give it your best shot and then carry on. It's as simple as that.

Finally, is this a "work" book or a "life" book? Good question. Exactly the question the publishers asked me when I first pitched it to them. *The Power Of Doing Less* assumes a basic view of the world where you have some kind of work you do and then that you also have a life outside work. Your work can be as an employee of any size organization, public or private sector; you can be self-employed; you can be full-time or part-time. But it's also a life book in the sense that you could apply its ideas in your work or in your personal life – or both. It's completely up to you.

"Life moves pretty fast. If you don't stop and look around once in a while, you could miss it."

[– *Ferris Bueller's Day Off*, 1986]

Chapter 1

THIS PROBLEM
IS **REALLY**
SERIOUS

KNOW WHAT "*KAROSHI*" MEANS?

On 30 November 2007 the Nagoya District Court in Japan accepted Hiroko Uchino's claim that her husband, Kenichi, a third-generation Toyota employee, was a victim of *karoshi* when he died in 2002 at the age of 30. He collapsed at 4am at work, having put in more than 80 hours of overtime each month for six months before his death. The week of his death, Mr. Uchino told his wife, "The moment when I am happiest is when I can sleep". He left two children, aged 1 and 3.

As a manager of quality control, Mr. Uchino was constantly training workers, attending meetings and writing reports when not on the production line. Toyota treated almost all that time as voluntary and unpaid. So did the Toyota Labour Standards Inspection Office, part of the Labour Ministry. But the court ruled that the long hours were an integral part of his job. On 14 December the government decided not to appeal against the verdict.

The word "karoshi" in Japanese literally means "death from overwork". The major medical causes of karoshi deaths are heart attack and stroke due to stress. The first reported case of karoshi was in 1969 when a 29-year-old male worker at the shipping department of Japan's largest newspaper company, died of a stroke. But it was not until the later part of the 1980s, when several high-ranking executives, still in their prime, suddenly died without any previous sign of illness, that the media began picking up on what appeared to be a new phenomenon. This new phenomenon was quickly labelled "karoshi" and was immediately seen as a new and serious menace for people in the workforce.

But it's not just Japan. The average full-time American worker gets an average of 14 vacation days per year but most only use 12 of those days. Research done by the Center For Work-Life Policy shows that more than 53% of workers regularly forfeit vacation days in order to spend more time working. Nearly half of working Americans take fewer than 10 days and about 25% of Americans *don't take any vacation at all*.

We can probably safely assume that these same workers spend some of the weekend working on stuff they've brought home or checking email or taking/making work-related calls. The most recent *American Time Use Survey*[1] shows that people with jobs worked an average of 7.99 hours per day, up from 7.82 hours in 2010. Not too bad, I hear you say. No indeed – except that that 7.99 hours is *every* single day of the week. The idea of working five days a week seems long gone.

And while we maybe tend to think of the United States as being a very work-centred culture, the USA is nowhere near the worst when it comes to working very long hours. The average American works 1,695 hours per year. But that puts it at only *#19* in the overall world rankings. The top 10 look like this:[2]

Ranking	Country	Hours worked per year
1	South Korea	2,193
2	Chile	2,068
3	Greece	2,017
4	Russian Federation	1,973
5	Hungary	1,956
6	Poland	1,939
7	Israel	1,929
8	Estonia	1,880
9	Turkey	1,877
10	Mexico	1,866

Looking at these figures it really would appear that we are headed for a place where life is going to be just about work.

But we already know all this from our own experience. We are busy in a way that our parents never were. Work intrudes into our personal lives in ways that were unimaginable just a few years ago.

If this wasn't bad enough, most of this increased workload is not by choice. Far from it. These days most of this workload comes with an implied threat that if we won't do it, then bad things – redundancy, outsourcing, downsizing, offshoring – will happen. Work seems to be consuming our lives, so much so that we are losing sight of what life is really about, of the things that really matter to us, whatever those might be – family, children, loved ones, hobbies, ambitions, hopes, dreams.

> "Most men live lives
> of quiet desperation."
>
> - THOREAU, American philosopher (1817–1862)

And while it's not often mentioned, it's worth saying how an awful lot of this extra time worked is a complete and utter waste. Bosses or employees who equate attendance with productivity are nuts. The notion that people can work continuous long hours over extended periods of time and still remain productive is laughable. While this may sound counterintuitive, if we think a little about it, we can see why.

[
Bosses or employees who equate
attendance with productivity are nuts.
]

First, it's important to distinguish between a "push" to get a job done, versus slogging through something with no end in sight.

A push to get a job done may be to solve a critical problem or to hit a particular milestone. Such a push can be a great thing. It can be great for morale and team building and produce extraordinary results.

THE DAMBUSTERS RAID – OPERATION CHASTISE

The famous Dambusters Raid during World War II[3] is a great example of a push to get a job done.

It was early 1943. The Germans had just been defeated at Stalingrad but D-Day was still more than a year away and victory in Europe more than two years away. Barnes Wallis, a British scientist and inventor, came up with the idea that if some of Germany's dams could be breached, the resulting flooding in the Ruhr Valley would cause massive damage to the German industrial capability.

The problem was to design a bomb big enough and deliver it close enough to the dam that when it exploded it would destroy the dam wall.

Inspired by what happens when flat stones are "skipped" across a lake, Wallis came up with the idea of a "bouncing" bomb. His experiments and calculations showed that if the bomb could be dropped from a precise height of just 60 feet, it would skip across the lake in front of the dam, strike the dam wall and then sink in close proximity to it before detonating. The problem then became one of developing and testing the bomb and training RAF pilots to deliver it under the exact conditions that Wallis had specified.

In the end, the bomb was made ready in just ten weeks. Then the specially trained flight crews of 617 Squadron flew their planes – at night – at tree top height over many miles of enemy held territory. They located the dams, dropped their bombs, breached two out of three of them and caused immense destruction as a result.

Extraordinary things can be done when people work against the clock to solve a particular problem. As you can see, pushes can produce amazing results. But that's not what we're talking about here.

Rather it's about what Kenichi Uchino in Toyota was going through: long hours day after day, week after week with – unlike a push – no end in sight, nor even a clear goal or objective. Why does this result in poor productivity? Why is it that the results achieved are out of all proportion (and not in a good way) to the effort put in? Have a quick think about it and you'll see why. Picture this.

You come in to work early in the morning. You left work late the previous night so you're now back where you were just a few hours earlier.

This is not the first day you've done this. You've been doing this for a while – quite a while. You've been working long days, maybe just grabbing a sandwich at your desk and not eating properly in the evenings, perhaps getting a take-out or throwing a frozen pizza in the microwave. You haven't been exercising. Nor have you been spending time with your loved ones. And you haven't been using the weekend to recover from all of this because you've been working the weekends (or at least some of them) too.

There's no end in sight. It's not like this is to achieve something special – this is just the way life is.

Now imagine how you'll spend your day. You know you're going to be working 12–15 hours that day, so you essentially feel like you've got all the time in the world. You'll linger over coffee. Somebody swings by for a chat, you're more than happy to chat with them. Or you'll maybe go seek out other people to socialize with. You'll spend time at meetings that ramble on and achieve nothing in particular because it doesn't matter – you've got all the time in the world.

Towards the end of the day, rather than start some important piece of work, you'll say, "Ah, I'll start that tomorrow when I'm fresh" and you'll tinker with some emails instead.

In short, productivity goes out the window.

Now contrast that day with a day where you work a brisk eight or so hours. And imagine that your day *has* to be limited to eight hours. Imagine that you've got the hottest date of your life at 7 pm that evening.

Now, how will you spend your time? You'll plan your day. You'll make a list of the stuff you absolutely have to get done so that you can walk out the door that afternoon. You'll give short shrift to trivial or unimportant things. You'll set yourself a deadline so that you can go home and pretty yourself up. Maybe you'll have some contingency in your plan – aiming to get out at 4 pm but absolutely no later than 5. This is so that if some idiot does spring a surprise on you and asks you to do something, you'll have the time to do it and still be able to get out the door on schedule. You'll be brusque with time-wasters so that you can keep your little plan for your day on track and get to your date on time.

And productivity? It's goes through the roof. Days like this are *hugely* productive.

Endless long hours	Normal working hours
Got all the time in the world – "If I don't get it done today, there's always tomorrow"	Have to get certain things done today
No life outside work	A life outside work
Often no clear goal or plan other than to work long hours	Very clear goal and a plan to get there
No differentiation between important and unimportant things – "I'll get to it eventually"	Focus on the important things
Constant time wasting	Very little time wasting
Physically unhealthy	Physically healthy
A sense of trying to clear a vast mountain of stuff	A sense of definite and consistent progress towards an end goal
Potentially very stressful	Low stress

So which of these days would you prefer?

Tom De Marco, in his book *The Deadline*,[4] talks about the effects of the pressure to work long hours. This is what he says:

- "People under pressure don't think any faster.
- Extended overtime is a productivity-reduction tactic.
- Short bursts of pressure and even overtime may be a useful tactic as they focus people and increase the sense that the work is important, but extended pressure is always a mistake.
- Perhaps managers make so much use of pressure because they don't know what else to do, or are daunted by how difficult the alternatives are.
- Terrible suspicion: The real reason for use of pressure and overtime may be to make everyone look better when the project fails."

So here is perhaps the most depressing aspect of all of this working crazy hours – that much of it is a waste, a complete and utter pointless waste. Why on earth then would you want to sign up for something like that?

But time management should sort out all of this.

Shouldn't it ?

Do Less – Turn Something Down At Work

If, as we've said, the problem is too much to do and not enough time to do it, then clearly, every time you accept something more, then you take the existing problem and make it even worse. So how about if you were to *not* take on something? In other words, somebody asked you to do something and you declined it.

So this is going to be your first test. Next time you're in work, your job is to turn something down. It can be big or small, trivial or hugely important, it doesn't matter. Your job is to pick one thing that day and decline it.

How will you do that? Well, ideally you figure it out. It isn't actually that difficult. But it you really – and I mean really – try and you can't find a way, then read Chapter 5 and it will tell you how. But I'd much rather – and it would be much better for you – if you figured it out for yourself.

"There is nothing so useless as doing efficiently that which should not be done at all."

[– PETER DRUCKER, Management writer and theorist]

Chapter 2

WHY TIME

MANAGEMENT COURSES
DON'T WORK

Do Less – Don't Sign Up For A Time Management Course For The Wrong Reason

Go on to Amazon and put in the search term "time management". How many results did you get returned? The day I did it, I got a staggering 104,247 results returned. This is not to mention the courses, training companies, time management "systems" and all the rest of it, that are abroad in the world. So with this abundance of time management tools available, why do we continue to get busier and even more overloaded? What's happening? I think you'd have to agree there's something not working somewhere.

Whenever I teach a project management course and talk about how to manage multiple projects simultaneously, I always start out in the same way:

"It's a time management problem. Get your training department to organize a time management course and you'll be fine." *Laughter.* (I'm obviously not going to get off that lightly.)

"Have you ever done a time management course?"

"Yes."

"So you don't have a problem – you can leave now." *Laughter again.*

"No, I'm serious. If you've done a course and done what it said, then you wouldn't have a problem . . . would you?"

"Hm, I suppose . . ."

"So it wasn't a very good course?"

"No, it was a great course. I learned good stuff like getting rid of time stealers and planning my day and the two-minute rule (getting something done and out the way if it can be done within a minute or two).*"*

"So what happened? If the courses were so good, why do you still have a problem with overload?"

"I fell back into my old ways . . ."

"I came back to work and it was okay for a week or two but then it just went back to the way it was before . . ."

"I didn't have time to implement what I learned . . ." (The old ones are best!)

What is interesting about all of these answers is that the people feel that *they* did something wrong. They failed in some way – falling back into their old ways or allowing work to overwhelm them or not finding the time to implement the time management techniques from the course.

In saying these things, these people are doing an injustice to themselves. Because they didn't fail. It wasn't something they did or didn't do. It was something else entirely.

So what happened?

Here's a way that you could think about or model the world. In any period of time – the rest of today or the rest of this week or this month or this year or even your whole life – there are a bunch of things that you will **have to do** – things like your job, the weekly shopping, mow the lawn etc. Think of them as a physical pile of stuff, like a pile of bricks.

Now place on top of that pile another pile of stuff. These are the things which, in the same period of time, you **like to do** and would like to do more of. Your hobbies or socializing or hanging out with your children or loved one, for example.

Next, place on top of that pile another pile of stuff. These are things you **hate to do** but you have to do them anyway. Paying your taxes, queuing at airports, being stuck in traffic and so on.

> *"It's easier to do trivial things that are urgent than it is to do important things that are not urgent, like thinking. It's also easier to do little things we know we can do, than to start on big things we're not so sure about."*
>
> - JOHN CLEESE

Finally, place on top of the pile a fourth pile of stuff. These are the things that you would **really love to do**. These are the things which, if you didn't have to bother with the pesky business of earning a living, you would be doing all the time. These are the things which, if you won the lottery, you would do. Learn to paint or become a rock guitarist or sail around the world or climb the seven tallest peaks on the seven continents or whatever. So there we have it — a great big pile of stuff towering up to the sky:

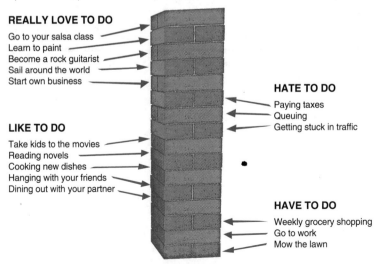

REALLY LOVE TO DO

Go to your salsa class
Learn to paint
Become a rock guitarist
Sail around the world
Start own business

HATE TO DO

Paying taxes
Queuing
Getting stuck in traffic

LIKE TO DO

Take kids to the movies
Reading novels
Cooking new dishes
Hanging with your friends
Dining out with your partner

HAVE TO DO

Weekly grocery shopping
Go to work
Mow the lawn

Now imagine a second pile of stuff. These are the things which, in the same period of time – the rest of today or the rest of this week or this month or this year or even your whole life – you **will actually do**. They are the things, drawn from each of the four categories, which will actually get done.

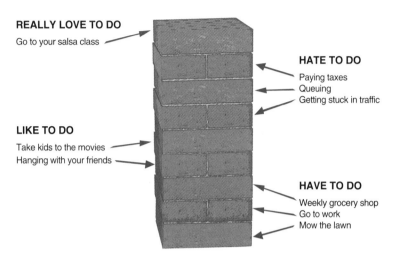

REALLY LOVE TO DO

Go to your salsa class

HATE TO DO

Paying taxes
Queuing
Getting stuck in traffic

LIKE TO DO

Take kids to the movies
Hanging with your friends

HAVE TO DO

Weekly grocery shop
Go to work
Mow the lawn

Do Less – Do Nothing For Two Minutes

Bizarre as it may seem, doing nothing can be difficult. Try the following for example and see how you get on. Visit this link http://www.donothingfor 2minutes.com/. Now just sit there and relax. Was it a blissful oasis of calm in a busy day? Or were you fidgeting after 30 seconds?

In general, for most people, the first pile of stuff is several, or maybe many times, higher than the second pile. Perhaps it has to do with how ambitious you are, or how driven you are. Perhaps it has to do with how organized or efficient you are. Perhaps it has something to do with your age – you reach a certain point in your life and you start to realize that life isn't infinite after all. You realize that if there are things you want to achieve in your life, you better start thinking of doing them now.

Now, if you go on a time management course or do what a time management book says, what will happen?

Well, it should have the effect of increasing the second pile (unless it's a particularly awful course or book). You will become more efficient. You will be able to get more stuff done.

Take something like the two-minute rule. David Allen mentions it in his very popular time management book, *Getting Things Done.*[5] We could imagine somebody who bought that book and just implemented that one idea, and would be able to increase the height of the second pile as little things whizzed across his desk and were dealt with.

But Allen's book or any other time management book or course isn't going to solve the basic problem that the first pile will still be many times higher than the second pile.

This is the problem with time management books and courses and systems. *They don't solve the right problem.*

> The problem with time management books and courses and systems is that they don't solve *the right problem.*

If you want to become more *efficient* and get more done, then time management will solve that problem. But that's not the problem most people have – or at least, it's not the most pressing problem.

The most pressing problem is that people have far more to do than they have time available to do it.

This then, is the reason why people report things like, "I fell back into my old ways" or "work overwhelmed me" or "I didn't have time".

Of course these things happened – because nothing had changed.

The first pile was still several times higher than the second pile.

The people who implemented what they learned on the time management course got a momentary "spike" or step-up of productivity that gave them the illusion that they had solved the problem.

But the problem remained.

The time management course hadn't solved it because this is not the problem that time management courses solve – even though, perhaps, they imply that they do.

And this is not to rubbish time management books and courses. They have their place and do useful things.

But they don't solve the problem you need to solve.

So if you're planning to spend your time and/or money on a time management book or course, just pause for a moment and ask yourself what problem you're trying to solve. If it's the problem of *efficiency*, i.e. you want to not waste time and get more done in the available time, then go for it. A time management course will do the business for you.

But if the problem you're trying to solve is too much to do and not enough time to do it, then forget about it. You'll just be wasting your time and money and you'll come away frustrated and feeling let down.

For *that* problem – too much to do and not enough time to do it – you need a different solution.

And before we talk about the solution, we need to talk about the *nature* of the solution.

Compare these two reviews of the book I mentioned earlier, one of the most popular and best-selling time management books of recent times, *Getting Things Done* by David Allen.

First, the bouquet: "This is a life-changing book. I was drowning in paper, felt constantly anxious about things I wasn't getting done, was missing deadlines, finding it hard to keep on top of my various commitments and projects. I thought I was just a disorganized person; this book has changed everything for me. I now have a clear idea of my commitments, an easy-access and reliable filing system, a simple way of capturing all my necessary actions, an empty inbox, and freer weekends." Wow!

Now, the brickbat: "I'll keep it brief because I'm guessing you're short on time – if only David Allen had done that. Instead this book is hundreds of pages of time management advice which, if you could take a year off to learn it, and then spend half your week organizing it as he suggests, it might all come together. David Allen has a knack of over-complicating things so adding complexity to an already busy schedule – no thank you!"

Same book!

So what's happening here? Maybe the bouquet-giver had a problem with efficiency, wanted to find ways to do more in the time he had available and therefore found the methods in the book particularly helpful. And perhaps the reason the brickbat did not find it as useful was because it wasn't actually solving the right problem for him.

More importantly though, what this also shows is that different things work for different people. The reason I mention this is to avoid falling into that trap in this book. Take what you will from the ideas in this book and see the various challenges as items on a menu. You don't have to try everything on the menu – just the ones that you like, that you find work for you.

If you've got too much to do and not enough time to do it, better time management is *not* the answer – you need a different solution.

Do Less – Turn Something Down In Your Personal Life

In Chapter 1, I asked you to decline something at work. Now try the same outside of work – at home or in your personal life. Again, you figure out how to do it and only if you're really, really stuck should you go to Chapter 5. As a possible hint, ask yourself whether the technique you used to decline something in the Chapter 1 exercise would also work here in this one. If it would, feel free to use it; otherwise come up with another one. And if you do come up with another one, would that technique also be usable in a work setting? If the answer to that is yes, then notice that you now have two viable techniques.

"Liberty means responsibility. That is why most men dread it."

[– GEORGE BERNARD SHAW   ]

Chapter 3

YOU WILL NEVER GET
EVERYTHING
DONE

There is a solution to the problem described in Chapter 1. And it's not time management courses or books. Instead, it comes with the realization of a simple but profoundly important fact.

You will never get everything done.

Let me say that again. You . . . will . . . never . . . get . . . everything . . . done.

You will never clear this mental (or written) list that you carry around with you. You will never make the first pile disappear. You must throw overboard, now and for all time, the notion that it is possible to do everything that needs to be done, to clear everything on the list. It simply is never going to happen.

Once you realize – and really internalize – the truth of this state-ment, a couple of very interesting things happen.

■ **Liberation**
You recognize, for example, that it's okay to leave work with things not done. There's no need to feel guilty about it. Not only is it okay, it's inevitable. It would be a miracle if you *did* get everything done. And it is liberation too in the more important sense of freeing up time. If you're not going to do everything then every time you decide not to do something, that time becomes available for something else. "Why should I invest my precious time in this?" is going to become one of your most asked questions.

■ **Responsibility**
In some ways, it's the easiest thing in the world to slug away at a list of things in the vain hope of trying to clear it. But now, if you're not going to clear it, you've got some major decisions to make. If you're not going to clear it, then what are you going to choose to do? Because now that's exactly what the problem becomes – which things are you going to invest your time in? Which

things are you going to disregard? And how are you going to make those choices?

> *"Beware the barrenness of a busy life."*
>
> - SOCRATES

Let's go back to our picture of the two piles of stuff from Chapter 2. How can you make the first pile "fit into" the second pile?

Well, here's what most people do. They try to "clear the pile". Very quickly they find that this doesn't work – which, of course, it can't.

So then they stop doing the:

And end up just doing this:

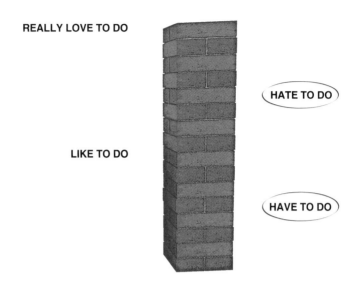

At this point they no longer have a work/life balance. They work continuous long hours and whatever home life they have is taken up with "noise" – the basic cooking, cleaning, shopping and general maintenance that keep our personal lives rolling along.

But then it gets worse than that. They continue trying to clear the pile, working even longer and longer hours and, in the process, destroying whatever precious hours of personal life they have remaining. But this is never going to work. As we have said before, you cannot clear the pile. It is a pointless, unwinnable game.

If you accept this idea, then logically you then have to accept that some things are *never going to be done*. Not delayed, not deprioritized, not left till later, not rescheduled, not done some day when you have time – but *never done at all*. Dropped. Ditched. Jettisoned. Made to go away. Forever.

Rather than trying to clear the pile – a pointless exercise anyway – we're going to do a much, much smarter thing. *We're always going to be doing the most important things.*

And how do we do that? Well, there's only one way.

[
You must learn to do less.
]

If you can do this then the right stuff will get done. And by "the right stuff", I mean that unique combination of things from each of the four categories:

- have to do
- like to do
- hate to do (but have to do anyway)
- really love to do

that's right for you.

I would probably be prepared to bet my house that this is the first time anybody has suggested anything like this to you – that there is, in fact, an essential skill that you are missing. Because if you think about it, right from the time you started school and maybe even earlier, you have been programmed to do exactly the opposite of this. People have told you to do stuff and you have done it.

Remember that first day in school. Your mum took you to the school, handed you over to the teacher and s(he) gave you bricks or plasticine or a colouring book and told you to do stuff with it. And being the well-balanced child that you were, you didn't tell them to bugger off, you did stuff. Then on through primary school and secondary/high school, you got assignments, homework, projects, continuous assessment, people getting you to do stuff. If you did some kind of third level education, the same thing – assignments, tutorials, end of term papers, projects, dissertations, theses. And maybe you had part-time jobs while you were in school or college and people told you to do stuff there and you did – wash glasses, wait tables and so on.

And then you began your first "real" job and what did you get? Job descriptions, objectives, key results areas, key performance indicators – always people telling you to do stuff. And basically – right up to the day they're going to haul you out feet first – that's probably the way you saw it being. People would be telling you do stuff and you would respond by saying, "How can I pack this in to an already overcrowded life?"

But if you can learn the skill of simply doing less – and it is a skill, just like using a computer or project management or chairing a meeting – you can not just tinker with the problem of too much to do and not enough time to do it. You can solve it.

THE GOALKEEPER THAT
STANDS STILL

Economist, Ofer Azar, knows all about doing less. Recently he and some colleagues in Israel published a study on goalkeepers[6]. They watched hours of archival footage and noticed that goalkeepers save substantially more penalty kicks when they stay in the centre of the goal than when they jump to the left or right. Yet paradoxically, in 93.7% of penalty situations, keepers chose to jump rather than stay in the centre.

In fact, analysis of 286 penalty kicks taken in elite matches around the world showed that keepers saved 33.3% of penalties when they stayed in the centre, compared with just 12.6% of kicks when they jumped right and 14.2% when they jumped left.

Or to put it another way, doing nothing would have achieved a far better result than doing something.

But notice too how hard it is to do nothing. Imagine if you were that goalkeeper and you stood stock still while the penalty taker rocketed the ball into the top corner. Imagine the abuse that would be heaped upon you by your teammates and by the fans. Imagine the embarrassment and guilt you would feel. Imagine trying to explain in an after match press conference that the reason you stood still was that, statistically, you were doing the best thing. It's like we would rather do something – anything – and be seen to fail rather than do nothing, even though we know it might be the better thing to do.

The book that you hold in your hand is called *The Power Of Doing Less*.

How can there be power in doing less? When we think of the word "power" we perhaps think of powerful people – the people who now or through history have shaped the world by the things they have done. Their lives have been characterized by action; their lives are known or remembered for their achievements – good or bad – but certainly things *done*. How could there be power in *not* doing things?

Well here's one for starters. There's a generally accepted view that when a new CEO joins an organization, what they *do* in the proverbial "first 100 days" will determine their ultimate success. (More generally, it's also become a bit of a staple of TV news channels to examine what new political leaders or governments have done in *their* first 100 days.) But if you're a CEO, this article from the *Harvard Business Review*, "Five Myths of a CEO's First 100 Days"[7] might give you pause for thought. The article says that perhaps a lot less doing and a lot more thinking might be a far more productive way to go.

Or think of a blogger pressuring himself to write a new blog post every day or so because isn't this what the social media experts say we should do? The same blogger might be far better off posting one decent article a week rather than cluttering up his life (and ours) with second-rate pap.

We're all guilty of doing this "busy" thing. Compulsively checking emails is a classic example. What on earth is the point in that? It's not like it's going to make the messages arrive any quicker.

HOW WORLD WAR I MIGHT HAVE
BEEN AVOIDED BY DOING LESS

On 29 June 1914 a Serbian terrorist assassinated the heir to the Austrian throne and the resulting sequence of events triggered World War I. There were numerous points in this train of events where things could have gone differently and war been avoided completely. One of these points occurred in late July.

After the assassination, Austria wanted to attack Serbia to teach it a lesson. Russia was Serbia's ally and it wanted to support Serbia. However, by this the Russians meant *diplomatic* support (and certainly not military intervention).

In these circumstances, all the Russians would have had to do would have been to sit tight and do nothing. The Austrians, unsure of the Russian's intentions, would have backed down and war would have been avoided.

As the historian A J P Taylor puts it[8] ". . . It never occurred to them [the Russians] that merely *by doing nothing* [my italics], they could prevent Austria acting against [i.e. attacking] Serbia . . . *The most difficult thing in a crisis is to wait upon events*" [my italics again].

> *"Besides the noble art of getting things done, there is the noble art of leaving things undone. The wisdom of life consists in the elimination of non-essentials."*
>
> - LYN YUTANG, Chinese writer

All of us lead busy lives. Maybe we fall into bed at night exhausted after the day with a feeling that we got lots done. Perhaps we *are* getting lots done.

But is it the stuff that really matters?

Or is it just *stuff*?

And does it matter which stuff, provided we are getting stuff done – working our way through this seemingly endless list of things that we have to do?

Well, of course it *does* matter.

So that if you're maybe feeling lost and a victim of the times and of circumstances, you have power.

You have power, if you will only take it and use it.

That power is to do less.

This book has a simple message. Whether in work or in your personal life, there is too much to do. The list is too long and will never be cleared – not even if you had several lifetimes to clear it.

Do Less – Let Go Of The Notion That You Will Get Everything Done

It's time to accept that you're simply not going to do certain things – many things, in fact.

Say it to yourself now. "I'm not going to do many things."

Repeat it a few times. "I'm not going to do many things." "I'm not going to do many things." "I'm not going to do many things."

Say it out loud. "I'm not going to do many things."

Do this now. Stand up. Picture, a pace or two in front of you, a doorway and a closed door. On this side of it is where you are now, the world of endlessly busy. The weather is grey over here, the landscape dully urban. A hamster runs round on a wheel. The hamster is you.

Now put your arm out – go on, do it – and push the door slightly. It swings ajar a little with no great difficulty. Looking through it you can see sunlight, green fields. You can hear laughter and smell nice smells – the sea, freshly cut grass, perfume.

This side of the doorway is where you are now. The Land of How-Can-I-Fit-This-In-To-An-Already-Overcrowded-Life? Step forward and step through the doorway. Come on – really – do it. Take the handful of steps needed to do it. Pass between the doorposts, under the lintel and step on into the other side. This is the Land of Why-Should-I-Invest-My-Precious-Time-In-This?

That wasn't too difficult, was it?

> "To comprehend a man's life, it is necessary to know not merely what he does but also what he purposely leaves undone. There is a limit to the work that can be got out of a human body or a human brain, and he is a wise man who wastes no energy on pursuits for which he is not fitted; and he is still wiser who, from among the things that he can do well, chooses and absolutely follows the best."

- JOHN HALL GLADSTONE, 19th Century British chemist

Here's another picture I want you to imagine. You're sitting in your seat slumped across your desk. Why are you slumped across your desk? Well, imagine your desk as being inside and at the bottom of, a giant silo or cylinder. What happens then is that people throw stuff in the top of the silo. Let's start at work.

Your boss throws stuff – requests to do things, projects, "this'll only take a minute" and so on. Your team, colleagues, peers throw stuff. Other departments throw stuff. Moving outside work to home, your wife/husband/girlfriend/boyfriend/partner/flatmates/housemates throw stuff. Your family throws stuff. The community in which you live and the government throw stuff. Other people throw stuff and last of all, you throw stuff yourself. All of this stuff comes raining down on your back. No wonder

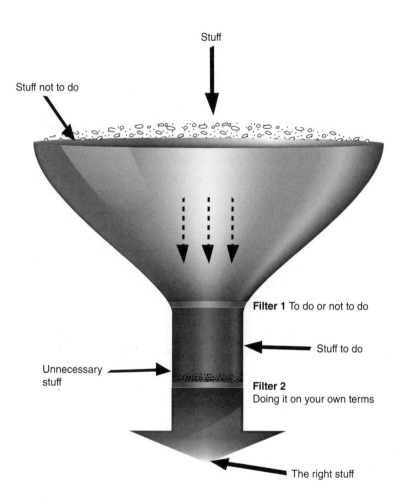

Stuff

Stuff not to do

Filter 1 To do or not to do

Stuff to do

Unnecessary stuff

Filter 2
Doing it on your own terms

The right stuff

you're slumped! It's a wonder any of us can get up in the morning.

But it's possible to have a different picture.

Instead of your desk being at the bottom of a silo, think of it as being at the bottom of a funnel.

The funnel has two filters in it. Exactly the same volume of stuff from exactly the same sources gets thrown in the top of the funnel. But this time it's filtered. Some things get stopped by the first filter so that only a smaller number get through. Some things get stopped by the second filter so that only a manageable number – the right stuff – get through. You're not slumped any more now. You're sitting up and you've got a smiley face ☺ because now you've got a life. Now the right stuff is being done. Imagine how happy you would be in those circumstances.

So obviously, we need to talk about what the filters are and we do that in Chapters 5 and 6. But first we need to talk about what constitutes "the right stuff".

And this time, just to finish off the chapter, we have a couple of "Do Less" challenges for you. Try these on two separate days.

Do Less – Decline Everything For Half A Day

Back to work again and your task is to decline everything for half a day. So for instance, you could decide to decline everything that everybody asks you to do all morning (i.e. up to lunchtime) or all afternoon (up to the time you go home).

In this exercise it's acceptable, for instance, to say all morning, "Can it wait until the afternoon?" Or to say, all afternoon, "Would it do tomorrow?"

While this doesn't get rid of the thing completely it does delay it. In addition, there's always the possibility that priorities will change and that you won't have to do it. (Or they might just forget about it! Nice.)

Do Less – Play The Declining Game For A Whole Day

Today, you want to make a game of declining things. Do this by declining – for a whole day – every second request that comes your way. You can use the techniques you've developed so far or try some new ones. How might you come up with some new techniques? Well, you can dream them up for yourself or ask other people. Ask your work colleagues at coffee break or lunch. Ask friends and family if they have good ways of saying no to things.

And what are you going to do if the greatest of all bosses is heading in your direction and it's time to say "no" nicely. Chicken out or go for it? As with all this stuff, it's your choice.

"Doing more things faster is no substitute for doing the right things."

[– STEPHEN COVEY, Motivational author and speaker]

Chapter 4

KNOWING WHAT THE **"RIGHT STUFF"** IS

The first step in learning to do less is to figure out what "the right stuff" is – the stuff that you're going to invest your precious life into. Only you can know what "the right stuff" is for you. Others may be affected by the choices you make but – ultimately – you have to decide what's right for you. And what's right for you will be as unique as you are. As a loose distinction, it's probably good to divide things up into "work" and "life" so we'll look at each in turn.

Also, at the end of this chapter, we'll talk in more detail about the two filters and what they are and do.

Work? A lot of it shouldn't be done!

In work, there's usually no shortage of people telling you what to do, and no shortage of ways for them to tell you. Requests, direct orders, objectives, key results areas, balanced score-cards, goals, targets, meeting action items and god knows what else. So there shouldn't be any great problem in work knowing what the right stuff is. Correct?

Er, well no actually.

Not quite true.

In fact, in my experience, not very true at all.

A friend of mine used to work for a big multinational bank. One day she told me she was being sent on a two-day training course on how to use the company's new performance appraisal system. When she came back she told about the system. It was a web-based, 360 degree appraisal. Your objectives went into the system. Then, when appraisal time came round, you appraised your boss, your boss appraised you. Your colleagues appraised you, you appraised your colleagues. Then all these appraisals were churned around, compared against the objectives and the answer came out – the answer to how your performance had been over the last twelve months.

Sometime after that again, my friend told me she was going to be having her annual appraisal.

"How are you going to do?" I asked.

"I don't know," she said.

I started laughing. I thought she was joking. When I saw that she wasn't, I said, "But what about the performance appraisal system, 360 degrees, web-based –"

"Yes," she said with a smile. "The fact is I don't know if I'm going to be rated 'meets expectations' or 'exceeds expectations'." Clear objectives? 'Fraid not.

There are many people that don't really know what their objectives are. Not really. Oh sure they have things like, "Get the projects done" or "Keep the customers happy" or "Make the world a better place for little furry animals" but as we'll see shortly, there is a big problem with objectives like these.

Here's one I came across recently. Somebody told me that their key objective for the year was to "be the voice of the customer".

"What does that mean?" I asked.

"Well, you know – to represent the customers' interests on the projects."

"Fair enough. So how will you know – when the end of the year comes that you've done a great job being the voice of the customer? And perhaps more importantly, how will your boss know?"

Long silence.

Some objectives are as I've just described. Some, on the other hand, are like the following – objectives of one of the people (let's call him Charlie) in ETP, my training and consulting company. They are:

- Do 75 days in front of clients, i.e. delivering training or doing consulting.
- Meet a monthly sales target of € 30,000 per month.

Can you see the difference? And can you see what the problem will be? In the second case, Charlie should only do things which contribute to one or other of his objectives. If something doesn't contribute to achieving the 75 days or the monthly sales target, then it absolutely shouldn't be done. Clearly Charlie would be nuts to do otherwise. Charlie knows with blinding, laser-like clarity what the right stuff is.

But in the first case – "be the voice of the customer" – who knows what the right stuff is? In this case, the person involved will work on certain things throughout the year. But are these *exactly* the same things that their boss reckons constitute being the voice of the customer? Highly unlikely, wouldn't you agree?

And this in turn means that you and your boss have two slightly (or could be *very*) different interpretations of what a good or a great performance would be. It's like this (not to scale) picture:

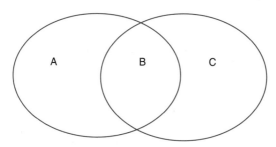

Your view   Your boss's view

What will happen then, is the following:

▨ You will spend some of your time doing the stuff in zone
B. This is value-added work in the sense that it definitely
makes a positive contribution to your end of year
performance assessment.

■ You will clearly spend time on the stuff in zone A since
– in your view – this is stuff that definitely matters. In
actual fact, this stuff is irrelevant and any time spent on it
is wasted.

▨ You won't do the stuff in zone C – basically, because
you don't know it has to be done. As a result of not
doing this stuff you're pretty much guaranteed not to
make your boss as happy as you might otherwise have
done.

Look at what this means – you (in all probability) bust your ass
– and for what?

When I teach this stuff to people I refer to it as "boxes":

"Meet a monthly sales target of € 30,000 per month"

and "clouds":

"Be the voice of the customer"

To know what the right stuff is at work, your objectives need to be boxes not clouds.

If your objectives are boxes, then fine and dandy. But what if they're not? What should you do then? Well, you need to go talk to your boss. And you need to have the conversation that begins with the words, "Hey boss, when the end of the year comes, how will we both know that I've done an amazing job?"

Before you do this, there's some preparation you would need to do. For those objectives of yours which are cloudy, you need to figure out some measures of them. These measures in turn, will make your clouds into boxes.

REMOVE THE CHICKENSHIT
FROM YOUR LIFE

If you've ever seen the miniseries, *Band of Brothers*[9] you'll remember from the first episode or two, the character Captain Sobel, played by David Schwimmer. In the book, *Band of Brothers*[10] Stephen Ambrose describes Sobel as "the classic chickenshit" and goes on to say, "he generated *maximum anxiety over matters of minimum significance*" [the italics are mine].

Paul Fussell in his book, *Wartime*[11] explains about chickenshit in the military. He says, "Chickenshit is so called – instead of horse- or bull- or elephant shit – because it is small-minded and ignoble and takes the trivial seriously."

Chickenshit isn't just confined to military. All of us have chickenshit in our lives – in work, absolutely, but also in our personal lives. All of us find ourselves taking "the trivial seriously" and "generating maximum anxiety over matters of minimum significance". The purpose of this book, and the power of doing less, is to remove most, if not all, of that chickenshit from your life. This chapter is a key step toward doing that.

I say that *you* need to do this because your boss almost definitely won't. Bosses have too much to do and not enough time to do it, just like everybody else – and so they're more than happy to go with the same old tired, cloudy objectives that have been passed along from one year to the next. So the chances are they won't make the first move. That means you have to. Propose some measures, go talk to your boss and either agree that your measures are okay or – even better – the pair of you, working together, come up with even better ones.

The result? You will now know what the right stuff is in work and you will be able to get that right stuff done, exceed expectations and all with the least amount of effort and wasted/misdirected time and energy.

And you'll also know what *doesn't* need to be done – and since we're interested in the power of doing less, this is what lights *our* fire. You are now saying that this stuff doesn't matter and it is never – and I repeat, never – going to be done. That feels good, doesn't it?

Do Less – Figure Out What Matters In Work

Start with any of your objectives that are fluffy, then replace them so that they can be boxes:

"Be the voice of the customer"

"Get input from a representative sample of at least 100 customers before finalizing the specification of any new product."

"Increase the accountability of Operations and reduce the need for QA second review and approval"

"Ensure that that the number of QA second reviews drops from x per week to y per week."

(Note too that it's okay to have more than one measure for an objective.)

■ At this point all your objectives should be clear and measurable. Now look at them in turn. For the measures of each particular objective, what would you and your boss class as a good/acceptable performance? This is the performance level that your boss is expecting and would get you whatever promotion or rise you are chasing at the end of the year. For example, suppose you have a sales target of € 30K per month that has already been agreed; then that is the acceptable performance level. Now what would be a really extraordinary performance level? Maybe in the sales target example, it would be € 40K per month. And finally, what would be an off-the-scale performance level? Maybe that would be anything more than € 50K per month. Do this in turn for each of your objectives summarizing them in a little table thus:

Priority	Objective	Acceptable Level	Extraordinary Level	Off-the-scale Level
1	Monthly Sales target	30K	40K	50K
2	Get input from a representative sample of at least 100 customers before finalizing the specification of any new product			
3	Ensure that that the number of QA second reviews drops from x per week to y per week			
4				

> *"It's not enough to be busy, so are the ants. The question is, what are we busy about?"*
>
> - HENRY DAVID THOREAU, American philosopher

Life? Don't miss it!

Did you ever think it would be great if you had some sort of Personal Life Objectives Fairy to tell you what to do with your personal life as well? Imagine it. Every year, on your birthday, this person would somehow show up and they would hand you your personal life objectives for the year ahead. Give up smoking. Join a gym. Spend more time with the kids. Get that guitar out of the attic and start practising again. And so on. Then they'd come back towards the end of the year and grade you. Met expectations. Exceeded expectations. Fired. Or whatever.

Fortunately or unfortunately, the Personal Life Objectives Fairy doesn't exist. You have to do that yourself.

So if you're unsure about what matters to you in life, then here's the quickest way to find out. (And after that there are some other ways that you can also try.)

Do Less – Find Out In Five Minutes
What Really Matters To You

1 Imagine you have somehow found out that you have exactly three months left to live. It's definitely true. There's no mistake. You're going to have 90 more days and then that's it. It'll be a wrap. Imagine it. *Really* imagine it.

2 Now give yourself five minutes (no more, no less) to make a list of all the things you would want to have or do or achieve or experience in those 90 days.

3 Now imagine you've been given a "get out" clause. Out of the list you've just made, if you can identify three things that you're prepared to put time into to make them happen, then you get to live until these three things are accomplished.

4 So identify those three things. Seems like these could well be the things that really matter to you.

Did you find that "Do Less" challenge difficult? If you did, you're not alone. It can be trickier than you think to identify the things that matter most to you.

So here's something else you can try. Imagine that you won the lottery. What would you do? The question is a cliché; the answers equally so. "I wouldn't have to work anymore." "I wouldn't have to worry about money." "I'd buy all this stuff – cars, houses, holidays, clothes . . ." "I'd never have to cook again." And so on.

Okay, fair enough. But assuming you did win the lottery, you're still going to have to find things to fill your days. After you've gotten up in the morning, *not* gone to work, checked your bank balance and seen the seven-digit figure there, surveyed your house, the cars in your garage and all your other "stuff", after you've eaten the healthy and gorgeous breakfast that was cooked and served up to you by your personal chef . . . what are you going to do then?

Knowing what you want to do with your life isn't something that everyone automatically knows. Some people do. I'm lucky enough to be one of them, for instance. For the last 30 years, consistently and without interruption I have wanted to be a writer. In fact, I have wanted to be a novelist. These days I spend some of my time doing that and I spend a lot of time writing. If I were to win the lottery, I probably wouldn't fill my days too differently from the way I fill them at the moment. There would probably be more writing fiction and less of the other kinds of writing. I might buy a new car but I'd be more likely to get my 1998 Saab Convertible fixed and back on the road. I might take a few more holidays/trips because I like travelling, and I might eat out a bit more, because I like food, and I'd definitely give more to charity but, other than that, I'm pretty happy that I have figured out what constitutes "the right stuff" for me.

Have you?

Because it's bloody important! It's clearly important in our working lives. But it's even more important in our lives generally. Life's not a rehearsal is a well-known saying. And indeed it's not. You get one crack at it.

So given that we only get one crack at it, we'd better make sure that we end up with the life we wanted and not some life that we feel was forced on us in some way or one that just sort of . . . well, happened to us.

Maybe you already know what life you want and if you do, that's great. But if you don't or you feel you've lost sight of it, then, apart from what we just did, there is a whole bunch of other ways to do it.

How would you like to spend your time?

It has always seemed to me that how somebody wants to spend their days and weeks and months is the best way of figuring out what they really want. If you can describe your ideal day, week, month or year, then you are a long way towards figuring out what you really want — what "the right stuff" is for you. So how are you going to do that? Take a look through the questions that follow and see where they take you. Write down your answers or anything else that occurs to you.

How much money would you have in your bank account?

Where would you be living? With whom?

What sort of house would you be living in?

Would you be working at all?

If you weren't working what would you be doing?

Would you have a commute to do or would you be working from where you live?

If you were working, where would you be working?

Who would you be working with?

How much money would you have in your bank account?

What would you be doing?

Would you be healthy?

What role would you have?

What things would you buy?

How would you know when you'd done enough work?

What type of things would fill your day?

Would weekdays be the same as weekend days?

How would you spend a typical evening?

Would you cook or go out to dinner?

Would you look forward to Mondays – or at least, not mind them?

How would you spend the weekend?

Would you be sorry to finish work on a Friday because you'd liked it so much?

Would you have more leisure time or "quality time" (with children or family or friends, say) than you do at the moment?

Would you be busier than you are at the moment? Quieter?

Would you be taking more holidays than you take now? If so, how much?

Are there people who are doing now what you'd like to be doing?

Do Less – Morph The Picture

So having answered these questions, you have a picture of how you would like life to be. There are things that exist now that you don't see in this new life picture. Look back over the notes you made and list what they are.

For instance, maybe you currently commute to work and in your new life you don't. Maybe there are people in your life now that aren't in the new picture. Maybe there is work you do now that doesn't appear at all in the new picture.

These things that don't exist in your "new life picture" are the things you need to do less of until eventually they disappear altogether. Write down what they are. These should be the first things that you target when it comes to the next part of the book.

SOME OTHER RESOURCES

As well as doing the things above, there are five other resources that I would highly recommend. Four are books which, if you want to:

- discover what your passion is
- start a business
- get the perfect job or make a career change
- change your life,

will do it for you. Respectively they are:

- *The Passion Test: The Effortless Path to Discovering Your Destiny*[13]
- *Wake Up and Change Your Life* [14]
- *What Colour Is Your Parachute*[15]
- *Awaken the Giant Within: How to Take Immediate Control of Your Mental, Emotional, Physical and Financial Destiny!*[16]

And if you're *really* serious about starting a business – and can afford it (and maybe even if you can't) – check out Marie Forleo's B-School: http://rhhbschool.com/.

The filters again

Hopefully by now, you should be really clear on what "the right
stuff" is for you. Now, all you need are the "filters" we spoke
about and you can start to get rid of all the stuff that isn't "the
right stuff". Imagine how enjoyable that's going to be.

So clearly, we need a filter to decide what we're going to do
and what we're not going to do. Furthermore, for the things we
decide *not* to do, we have to have a way of "killing" them. If
we can't do that then they will keep bobbing around and tor-
menting us. Both of these things make up this first filter.

And then, for the things we *do* decide to do, we want to do
them with the least amount of effort – by which we mean as
efficiently as possible with minimum firefighting and nasty surprises. We call this "doing things on your own terms".

Here they are then – the two filters:

1 One to determine what to do and what not to do – and as part of that, to "kill" the things we decide not to do
2 One to get the things we do decide to do, done on our terms.

These in turn, will enable us to do "the right stuff". Problem solved.

The filters are described in the next part of the book so let's go. Oh and here's a "Do Less" to keep you entertained today.

Do Less – Did You Do "The Right Stuff"?

Today, at the end of your day, look at things that you actually got done. Do you think they were "the right stuff"? If not, why did you do them? And next time out, what would you do differently to avoid doing them?

Spend a little bit of time on this. It would be good to write down your thoughts.

"The key is not to prioritize what's on your schedule, but to schedule your priorities."

[– STEPHEN COVEY, Motivational author and speaker]

FILTER ONE –
TO DO or
NOT TO DO

If we are to do the right stuff, then we need to filter out anything that isn't. And we want to do this both in work and in the rest of our lives.

Filter #1 is where we do this – where we make the crucial decisions about what to, and what not to, invest our precious time in. This filter says that we need to learn to prioritize viciously. As we will see, this will result in some things going through the first filter and some things being stopped. For the things that get stopped, we need to have a way of making them disappear so that they don't continue to annoy us. We discuss these two things in turn.

Prioritizing viciously

Let's get prioritizing out of the way first because I think there's some confusion about what this really means. Sometimes you hear people say "I have 5 priority one things to do, 17 priority two things and 49 priority three things to do". That's *not* prioritizing.

Prioritizing is taking a list of things to potentially be done and saying, "If I could only do one thing on this list, what would it be?" That then becomes your #1 priority. You then take the remaining list and ask the question again. "If I could only do one thing what would it be?" That becomes your #2 priority. Then you take the remaining list, ask the question again, and so on until the list is prioritized. Thus, each item is either more important or less important than each other item and you can't have a joint priority – a 7A and 7B, for example.

What this means in reality then, is that some things are wildly, massively, unbelievably important and lots of stuff . . . well, just isn't. So what you do is this:

Divide what you have to do into what's wildly important and what isn't.

(You will probably need to) agree this with somebody else. In work that person is likely to be your boss. Outside work, it could be the person/people you live with.

Prioritize the stuff that's wildly important.

Make the other stuff disappear – as we'll describe later in the chapter.

And then how do you make it work? How do make sure that you stick to doing just the right stuff? And what happens if someone challenges what you should and shouldn't do? Maybe your partner keeps asking you to do something that you believe is not a good use of your time. Or your boss gives you a task that you think won't really add any value. There are two things you need to do then, on an ongoing basis. You must:

- Consciously stick to only doing the "right stuff".
- Continually question what that "right stuff" is.

Consciously stick to only doing the "right stuff"

When you're asked to do something – be it at work or in the rest of your life – that is wildly important, you give it time, energy, commitment, skill, expertise, knowledge, passion, goodwill, love even – all that good stuff that you're capable of.

However, if the thing you're being asked to do is not on your wildly important list, then you make it disappear. Religiously. Every time. And you need to be strict about this. Don't wimp out. And if anybody complains or has a problem with this, you say quite clearly, "I explained – we agreed – these things matter, these things don't matter".

Continually question what that "right stuff" is

Okay, so you're making a conscious effort to just do the right stuff. But there's still more you can do to tighten your focus onto only doing the things that truly matter.

There will be some stuff on your wildly important list that will clearly always be there. In my project management business, for example, I have just two priorities – in the order shown:

1 Delivering services to existing customers.
2 Bringing in new business.

These are never going to change as long as I continue to do this job. And it wouldn't make sense for either of them to be dropped from my list. These will always be my wildly important things. And you will have similar things on your list that are no-brainers.

But there may be other things on your list that you're not so sure about. You suspect that even though they might seem important, they may not be: you're not convinced. Your theory is that they don't really add value and are not a good use of your time. Or it may be that your boss, for example, has decided that *everything* you do is wildly important.

In either of these cases, here's what you can do. You want to test your theory. You want to prove for once and for all, whether something is wildly important or not.

The only way you can truly test whether something is wildly important is to *not* do it — and see what happens. If the sky falls, then clearly it was important. If it doesn't, then it wasn't. So here are some ways you can do that.

[If the sky falls, then clearly it was important.]

Start with the things that have the lowest priority on your list. Let's say that there's a meeting you go to every week and you're not convinced that attendance there is a good use of your time. Now let's be clear, I'm not saying that all meetings are a waste of time. Some meetings are immensely useful, solve problems, move projects forward, take decisive action and so on. But I think I'd have to say that, in my own experience, about 80% of the meetings I've been to over the course of my life have been a complete and utter waste of time. But maybe that's just me.

Also, let's be equally clear — the reason we're proposing to opt out of this meeting is not so that we can simply skive off. It's that we think the meeting is not a good use of our precious time and that we're proposing to reinvest that time into something more useful and important.

Anyway, back to your meeting. If you think the meeting might not be a good use of your time, then don't go. Notice too that there are many ways not to go to a meeting:

- The absolutely best way is to say you won't be able to attend because you're doing this other, more important thing instead. (And you could ask if somebody could take notes on your behalf.)
- Another good way is to be upfront and have a quiet word/send a message to the person running the meeting or to your boss explaining why you think it is not a good use of your time.
- You could also say, "Can I do my bit first?" and then leave.
- Or you could say, "Call me if you need me".

Okay, so you don't go to the meeting. As a result of this, one of two things will happen. Either the sky will fall – because the meeting *was* incredibly important and your attendance there was crucial . . . or else it won't. If the sky fell, then you have your answer. But if the sky didn't fall, then it means you got back a tiny piece of your precious life for something more important. More significantly though, this means that your presence at the meeting maybe isn't all that important. And since there is now a precedent for you not going, you can not go again. And maybe over time, your little victory becomes a much bigger victory as you stop going to that meeting altogether.

"A LOT OF PEOPLE THINK I'M A LAZY BUM!"[17]

The quote is from Daniel Day-Lewis, widely regarded as one of the greatest screen actors in the world. Yet in the last sixteen years he has only made six films. He says of the long periods he spends between films: "It's that period of time that allows me to do the work [the film making]. So these two things [the filming and the breaks between filming] are indivisible. They're part of the life that allows me to explore the work in a way that satisfies me."

He does less (the breaks between films) so he can do more (the extraordinary performances he gives in his movies). (And if you're unconvinced about this, go see Steven Spielberg's Lincoln.)

Suppose there's a report you do every week or month and you're not convinced that people read it. (Again I'm not saying people shouldn't write reports. Some reports provide vital information to the organization. But lots of reports get written just because . . . well, they've always been written.) So don't send it out and see how long it is before anybody notices. Suppose it's a weekly sales report sent to a team and it's ten days before you receive a message from somebody asking where the sales update is. First, this suggests that issuing the report once every couple of weeks would be sufficient. Second, maybe the person who chased after ten days is the only person who needs to receive it. So as well as freeing up another bit of precious time, you have also found out what is important (or not so important) to somebody else.

Yet another example of testing the boundaries is that there may be something that is part of your job that has been done a certain way for as long as anyone can remember. In our company, for example, we once had the Monday morning sales meeting. This was a *terrible* meeting. First of all it was first thing on Monday morning. Second, it was about sales and if sales weren't going well, that coupled with it being a Monday morning was enough to depress anybody. Finally, there could be up to ten people at it and it regularly lasted two to three hours. Eventually, we gave up on it. We found a different, far less time-consuming way of achieving what the Monday sales meeting achieved.

Finally, all of this shouldn't be just confined to work. As we've seen, work contains a whole bunch of stuff that doesn't matter that much. But this has to be even more true of life outside work where there is so much "noise" in our lives these days. The endless usage of social media, keeping up with your favourite TV programmes, having to manage all the details of family life, just the bare necessities of keeping the domestic show on the road – cooking, cleaning, shopping, chores etc.

Lots of the things that soak up our time should not be done. As always, let me be clear. I'm not encouraging anyone to live in squalor or not take care of their families. But I'm not the first person to point out that it doesn't actually matter if the house doesn't get vacuumed every day or the kids don't have a bath every single night, or that the world won't actually stop turning if you miss an episode of your favourite TV soap opera or don't get time to read that morning newspaper you bought.

I remember when I first got married, my wife and I used to do a supermarket shop every week. By the time we got there, had done what we had to do and got home, it had generally wiped out a Saturday morning. Not only that, it wasn't that much fun, trawling around a vast supermarket and then joining the inevitable long queues as everybody else did what we were doing. Over a month, these Saturday mornings amounted to two and a bit full days. And not any old days but weekend days – in some ways, the most precious days of all.

We eventually wised up. We switched to a supermarket shop once a month. Then, each day, one of us would pick up any things that we needed. Generally these were fresh things like meat, fruit, vegetables. We would buy these in a local market or corner shop or some specialist shop.

The result? First of all, we saved the best part of two weekend days a month. Second, we ended up throwing out a lot less stuff because it had gone past its use-by date. And finally, we ate and drank much better because we found all kinds of interesting shops and things in those shops. (I lived in France for eight years and there, most people shop for food every day. The French have got that right.)

There's a lot of living to be done. Don't let all this other stuff get in the way.

So, in summary, whether in work or in life generally, if there are things that you believe are not a good investment of your time, test your theory. You'll soon find out and may be able to push some things from the "Wildly Important" list to the "Isn't" list and every time you do that, it will be a sweet little victory indeed.

Making it happen

Ultimately, it's going to be what you do or don't do every day that determines the success of all this. So in the box that follows is the way to make sure that each day works out as you wanted it to. (If you're familiar with and use Stephen Covey's "first things first" and the "four quadrants",[18] then that would also achieve the same result for you.)

DO LESS – Plan Your Day to Get the Right Things Done

At the end of each day (i.e. last thing before you go home), take your list of things to have to be done tomorrow and categorize them according to this scheme:

Do Less – Say No in Work and in Life

For the next week, say no religiously to the things that are not wildly important. Every time you succeed, chalk up a little victory. Every time you fail, ask yourself why you did and figure out how you're not going to do so next time.

A – I have to do this tomorrow. I cannot go to bed tomorrow without this thing having been done. Planets will collide; stars will fall if I don't get this thing done.

B – It would be nice to get this done tomorrow but I don't have to.

C – Realistically, I'm not going to get this done tomorrow.

D – I can delegate it. It gets done and you don't do it. Nice!

Then, when you get in tomorrow, do all the D's, all the A's, and go home.

"What about the B's?", I hear you ask. "Never put off till tomorrow what can be done today." Isn't that the old saying? Well, actually on this one, Thomas Jefferson, to whom this is credited, got it wrong. Here's a much smarter analysis. If it didn't have to be done today, then it lies in the future. If it lies in the future, there's always the possibility that things may change and that it will turn out we don't have to do it. And what a tragedy then to have put our precious time into it. Now admittedly, this doesn't happen very often but how sweet when it does.

Two further points here, just to round this off. What happens if the end of the day comes, you're going home and one of your A's wasn't done? Then clearly, it wasn't an "A" in the first place. The more severe/ferocious you can be when choosing A's, the better this will work for you.

And what happens if something new comes in during the day? Well then, you need to categorize it as an "A", "B", "C" or "D" and act accordingly. (But don't forget that there's always the possibility to negotiate it and trade it for one of your existing A's – "I can do this (the new thing) but then I can't do that (an existing thing)".)

Making things disappear

Remember that picture we had back in Chapter 3 with all the stuff we're asked to do going in the top of the funnel? The stuff that doesn't make it through the first filter has to be made to disappear. If it doesn't, we can picture it eventually clogging up the mouth of the funnel.

The way you're going to make it disappear is in the simplest way imaginable – you're just going to say "no" to it. To be precise, you're going to say "no" *nicely* to it.

I teach an online course on *The Power Of Doing Less* and here's what one participant emailed me recently on this issue of saying "no" and the liberation that comes with it. "I found myself declining a 3 hour each way road trip with 3 kids under 6, and soon after, a 2 hour each way version of the same, just half an hour ago. Love that feeling of relief!"

Paradoxically – and contrary to what you might have expected – not doing something requires work. That work comes from having to make the thing disappear. What we want though, is for the amount of work required to make it disappear to turn out to be far, far less than the work that would have been required, had we done it.

Some things should not be done at all. However, it's not enough to say we're not going to do it. We need to find a way of making it disappear so that it doesn't keep bobbing around and causing us to have to deal with it over and over again.

[Some things should not be done at all.]

The way to make something disappear, is to say "no" nicely to it

"I can't do that 'for personal reasons'."

"That's not really my area of expertise." / "Charlie would be a better man to do that."

"Can you let me think about that?" (And – ideally – hope it goes away.)

"No thank you."

"I can't do that because I'm left handed!"

"I can do this (the thing you're being asked to do), but then I can't do that."

"You're going to have to talk to my boss about that."

"That's not part of my job description."

"I'm kinda busy or gotta deadline (or whatever) at the moment – could you come back to me about that say, tomorrow?"

"I've got a work/home thing to do."

"I've got a headache."

"Why don't we do something fun instead?" (More for use in your personal life than at work!)

"I don't have the time."

"I'm sorry, I wouldn't be comfortable doing that."

"Sorry, we've got a prior engagement/other plans."

"That's not one of my priorities at the moment."

"I won't be able to do that any time soon."

"It'll be next week (or whenever) before I can get to that."

Ways to show you don't want to be disturbed

Buy or make a sign that says "Your lack of planning is not my emergency" and hang it up in your office. (I have actually seen some somebody walking towards somebody's cubicle, seeing that sign and then veering away!)

Go somewhere where you won't be disturbed. The absolutely best way to do this is to find some place where people don't expect you to be. Your hope is that "out of sight, out of mind" will occur and they won't ask you to do things as a result. This then means that you can spend the time you gain on important things. So – go to another part of the building, another floor, a different section or department. Book a conference room and work from there. Work from the coffee room/cafeteria/restaurant. Work in a nearby coffee shop, if there is such a place. Work from home, if that's an option. And if it's not, start to agitate to make it one.

Close your door. This assumes (a) that you have a door and (b) that it's usually open so that when it's closed, people know there's something serious going down.

Put on a pair of headphones while you sit at your desk.

Don't answer your phone.

Pretend you're out. "Stop, drop and roll" as someone I loved used to say – this for callers at your front door.

Divide the day up into periods of red time (say 10:00–12:00 and 14:00–16:00). Then, if somebody comes to you at 9:50, you give them 10 minutes of your time, energy, commitment, "Sit down, what can I do for you?" kind of thing. Somebody comes at 10:00; you ask if they could come back at 12:00.

When somebody comes to interrupt you, say, "I'm really involved in this at the moment"/"I have a really tight deadline" (irrespective of whether you do or not)/"I'm really trying to get my head around this problem right now"/ "I'm trying to split the atom at my desk"/whatever – "is there any chance you could come back in an hour?" In my experience, almost everybody respects this, nobody takes offence and guess what? Well, sometimes they don't come back at all! And sometimes when they do come back, they have several things they want to talk to you about. (I think we all know people who could be described as "serial interrupters".)

Only check your email once or twice a day. This is a well-worn piece of advice, as is turning off the thing on your computer that goes "bing" every time an email arrives.

Ways to sift out the timewasters

Write an out-of-office that reads something like this. "I'm going on holidays and won't be back until <date>. When I come back, I'll be emptying the contents of my inbox. So please contact me on my return." (Life *is* actually too short to go through several hundred emails, most of which are no longer relevant.)

Say, "Could you send me an email on this?" This, for example, is what support desks do all the time – the idea of "take a ticket". This is the first test they're setting you, to see how serious you are about your problem. If somebody isn't prepared to write you an email about something, you can fairly safely assume that the thing is probably going to go away.

Say "sure" and then do nothing – on the basis that if it's important they'll ask again (or come and check how it's going or something like that) and if it's not, then clearly it is something that can be resolved without you.

Don't return a missed call if the caller hasn't left a voicemail. It's clearly not that important.

Show them how overloaded you are. If you're interested, email me and I'll send you a simple Excel tool for calculating this.

Rather than simply saying "yes" to anything, aim to question the deadline given to you every time. Double the deadline and ask, "Would that do?" So, for example, somebody comes to you at noon and says, "Could you have that by close of business today?" ask, "Would it do tomorrow morning?" Or somebody says, "Could you review that sometime over the next week?" say, "Not sure if I could get to it in a week. I could do two weeks". You'd be astonished how often people say, "Yeah, that's fine – thanks". And we've all had the experience of busting our ass to get something done only to find the person for whom we did it saying, "Yeah, great. That's great. It would have done next week, though".

Deal with an email only once. Do one of four things to it – reply, forward, file, delete. Don't leave it languishing in your inbox were it will only continue to torment you.

A good friend of mine told me this. I pass it on and you can make up your own mind about it. I'd suggest it's a very extreme measure for very extreme circumstances. (My friend has only done it *once*, for instance.) Declare email bankruptcy i.e. send out a blanket message (like an Out Of Office response) saying the server died and you have lost everything. Tell your contacts that if they had a high-priority request with you to please resend it and you will address it as soon as your system has been restored. The *one* time my friend did this returned a 90%+ reduction in "demands". Most of the emails he got were ones of condolence!

WANT TO BECOME RICH?
DO NOTHING

Want to become rich like Warren Buffett? The billionaire investor and chairman of Berkshire Hathaway is well known for this piece of advice: "Don't sell your stocks. Instead buy and hold."

Buffett reckons that people sell stocks far too quickly and for all the wrong reasons. Rather than thinking like investors, they jump from sector to sector and stock to stock in the hope of making a quick killing, all the while trying to avoid being dashed on the rocks.

The trouble with this kind of trading is that the cost of so much activity wipes out any chance the investor has of reaping the rewards of owning the stocks. To invest like Warren Buffett, you have to get to that point where you *can* reap the rewards – which can take time.

When his stock is undervalued Buffett *does nothing*; he holds onto it rather than sells. This approach has made him richer than Croesus.

WHAT IF YOUR JOB IS COMPLETELY UNPREDICTABLE?

You may be one of those people who is in a very event-driven job. By this I mean that much of your time is spent responding to unpredictable requests that come in to you. Maybe you (wo)man a helpline or support desk. Or maybe you manage a team of people who can come to you out of the blue with queries or issues.

People in such jobs tend to say that saying "no" nicely is not for them and they just have to deal with everything that comes along. That may be true but there are still things you can do to get more control over what you put your time into. So if you're a person who is in such a job, this one is especially for you – because . . . it's possible to plan for the unexpected.

Really?

Yep. And you could start right now.

Each day for five days, record how much of your time goes into these interruptions. Let's say it looked something like this – in hours:

Mon	Tue	Wed	Thu	Fri
5	3	3	2	7

Add these hours up and you get 20. Divide by 5 (the number of days in the week) we get 4. So this says that on average you spend four hours a week dealing with interruptions. So plan for that from now on. Put four hours in your schedule every day for dealing with interruptions. (And keep track of it because maybe it varies over time. Maybe it's seasonal or to do with certain time of the month/year/quarter.) If you know that some of your time every day is going to go on interruptions, the daftest thing of all is to pretend that the time for dealing with interruptions is zero.

I recommend this hugely to anyone in such a job.

[
Deal with an email only once. Do one of four things to it – reply, forward, file, delete.
]

Do Less – Practise Saying "No" Nicely

Choose five ways of saying "no" nicely. Try to implement each of these at least once over the course of one day.

" 'It just shows what can be done by taking a little trouble,' said Eeyore. 'Brains first and then hard work. Look at it. That's the way to build a house.' "

[– A.A.MILNE, *The House at Pooh Corner*]

Chapter 6

FILTER TWO –
DOING IT ON
YOUR TERMS

We spoke about liberation early on in the book. I hope you can see how filter #1, To Do or Not To Do, delivers that liberation to you. Every time you say "no" to something that doesn't matter, you free up time for the things that really do.

Apart from the extra time you're finding every day, you should now also be feeling (or rediscovering) some new feelings. For one, you should be experiencing a greater sense of clarity. Before, it may have seemed like there was just one great big list of stuff that you had to slog away at in the hope of clearing it. Now, you see that some things matter hugely and lots of stuff is actually irrelevant. And every time you invest time in, and progress, something that matters hugely, you are – in a very real sense – living the life you are meant to live.

In work you should be experiencing a new sense of job satisfaction and creative freedom. You're getting to spend time on the things that count and doing them really well. You're getting time to draw breath, to think, to be creative. You've rid yourself of the useless and pointless to focus on what your job is really all about. You're delivering a far better performance for the hours you invest – you're getting maximum "bang for the buck". And this should be noticeable to you, your boss and the other people with whom you deal.

In your personal life, you should be feeling that this is much more how you wanted your life to be. Some people report a feeling of "it doesn't get any better than this" at this point.

So you can see that while, at first glance, this filter may seem very simple, it does, in fact, give you immense power. And if this book were to somehow end right now, you would have everything you needed to make huge changes in your life.

But we're not finished yet. We have one more weapon in our arsenal. And this one is a real zinger. It's going to ensure that when you do something, you do it:

- As efficiently as possible.
- With the least amount of wasted time, effort, energy, resources, money.
- With as few nasty surprises as possible.
- With minimum firefighting.
- And with minimum stress.

We call it "Getting Things Done on Your Own Terms".

WAIT UNTIL THE BASS BITE

Many anglers think that by moving the bait around, by being "active", they increase their chances of catching something. However, if you want to catch bass, the best way is by "dead sticking". Dead sticking quite simply involves casting the bait into the water and then letting it sit there . . . and sit there . . . and sit there. Frustrated anglers thrash about without making a catch. But the wise angler lets his lure sink to the bottom and allows the line to go slack. The angler then has nothing to do but wait until the bass bite.

Getting things done on your own terms

Let's look first at the things you can get asked to do – the "requests" that come to you. In work, they can range from "Would you mind taking care of this little thing?" right up to "I'd like you to run the X Project". But whether it's a tiny thing or a full-scale, cast of thousands project, that request almost always comes packaged with some constraints.

Constraints are things like "I need this by four o' clock today" or "I'm giving you the X Project. The budget's already been fixed at two million and you're going to have to do it with your existing team" or "The scope of this project has been agreed with the customer and the date Sales gave them was 30 September". You know the kind of thing.

It's fair to say too that these constraints may be self-imposed. In work, there may be a culture of "we can't say no", which you feel pressurized by. Outside of work, you may feel certain obligations to march to somebody else's tune – to do things that "they" want you to do.

The first thing you have to realize is that you don't need to agree to these constraints. This is especially true at work. If you do agree and the constraints turn out to be impossible to achieve, you're going to end up in a hell of a mess. You'll work nights, weekends, cancel holidays, you'll be stressed and work will be consuming all your time. Not only that, you may do all of the preceding and still find that the constraints were impossible to deliver. A huge expenditure of money, resources, time, energy, stress and your time – and for nothing. In short, the very opposite of what we're trying to achieve with this book.

So here's a piece of advice. Stop treating these constraints as though they came from God. Because this is exactly what we do. In work especially. We're told something like, "I want it by four o'clock today" or "It has to be done by the end of the quarter" and we treat these requests as though it had almost religious significance. So stop thinking of them like that. Think of them instead as a letter to Santa Claus.

[
Think of requests as a letter to Santa Claus.
]

To explain: We've all written letters to Santa Claus, where we've said, "Dear Santa, this is the stuff I would really like for Christmas". But how many times have we come scampering down on Christmas morning to find that we got some things but didn't get others? Because the world simply isn't like this, one where we can say "This is what we want" and it just happens.

The world of work is no different. Yes, our bosses or other people may want certain things. Yes, there may be perfectly good business reasons why they do want those things. But if the things they're asking for can't be achieved, we need to tell them that and then tell them then what *can* be achieved.

And all of the preceding applies in our personal lives as well. Yes, there may be things we want to achieve – move to a different house, buy a new car, go on a holiday to some place we've always wanted to go to, start our own business – and we will have set our own constraints on those. But again we need to know whether or not these constraints are achievable.

Maybe, for example, you've always wanted to start a business but you feel that without a lump of capital to start out with, you can't do it. However, today more than ever, the barriers to starting a business are low indeed. Many businesses – especially online ones – can be started with a derisory amount of money. (I started my business with a € 50,000 *debt*! While I'm not recommending this (!) it does show that self-imposed constraints – also known as limiting beliefs – can often be made to fade away.)

The way we're going to do things on our own terms is by building a plan, agreeing it with whoever we need to agree it with and then executing the plan.

Maybe, some time in your life, you've heard somebody say "We don't have time to plan it, just do it". This is always the wrong thing to say. If you don't build a plan you will spend/ waste more time, effort, resources and money in getting the project done – sometimes vast amounts of these things. Filter #2 essentially says that a little planning always beats a lot of firefighting.

And in case phrases like "spending all our time planning", "we can't plan for every tiny eventuality", "if we spend all our time planning, we won't have any time left do the project", "paralysis by analysis" and similar are starting to jump around in your head, don't worry. We're not talking about ridiculous levels of planning. Rather, it's about just enough to make sure you don't end up making rash decisions and commitments and getting yourself in a mess.

[A little planning beats a lot of firefighting.]

Why is planning such a good idea?

Imagine this. It's about six o'clock in the evening and you suddenly realize you're hungry and you decide to cook dinner. Imagine then you do the following:

1 Light the gas ring.

2 Look in the fridge to see if there is something to cook.

3 You find there's nothing that you like there, so you decide to head down to the supermarket. Hopefully, you turn off the gas ring before you go.

4 You return with some eggs. You're going to make an omelette.

5 You light the gas ring again.

6 Where's the frying pan? Uh oh, it's in the dishwasher and the dishwasher is part way through its cycle. Okay, let's wait until the cycle is over. Turn off the gas again.

7 Finally the dishwasher cycle is over and you starting cooking your omelette. But then you think "It'd be really nice to have some fried potatoes with the omelette". But, oh hell, you should have done the potatoes first because they take longer than the omelette.

8 You finish the omelette and put it in the oven to keep it warm. You start on the potatoes. You're going to have a can of mushy peas with them and happily, you have both the potatoes and the mushy peas.

But mid way through frying the potatoes, you change your mind. Wouldn't asparagus be really nice instead of mushy peas? Back down the store again.

And so on . . .

And of course nobody, except perhaps Mr Bean, would do this. Instead we do some organizing first. We make sure we have the ingredients and the equipment necessary to cook them. We also make sure we have a recipe – either in our heads or from a book. This recipe tells us what must happen in what order. With this organizing done, our cooking should go relatively smoothly. Our dinner should be ready in the shortest time and we shouldn't have too many things go wrong.

In the first scenario, you'd probably be lucky if you ate dinner at all that evening. And that approach would definitely have cost you more in terms of time, effort, energy, money and general overall stress.

And I don't know what your experience has been but mine has been that many, many work and home-related projects get done exactly like the cooking-the-omelette scenario. Rather than build a plan, people just launch into the project and the results are often disastrous.

So that is why we plan.

How do we plan?

Whether in work or in life generally it all begins with a request to do some project or other. That request may come from other people or it may be initiated by ourselves.

With other people, it's often things like "Can you do this thing for me" or "I'm giving you the X Project" – and by the way, here are the constraints. Typical constraints are:

- The time or date by which it must be done.
- The budget.
- Restrictions on resourcing/manpower.
- The scale of the thing has already been decided.
- Or some combination of these things.

If the request was initiated by ourselves then we set the constraints ourselves. For example, we might decide that we want to get the house redecorated in time for Christmas or put down a patio or lawn before the summer comes.

And we mentioned already how some constraints can act as limiting beliefs. Limiting beliefs are really bad news since they can severely hamper our ability to live the life we want to live. While dealing with such beliefs is outside the scope of this book, you don't necessarily need a therapist to help you get past such beliefs. Planning can provide a simple and massively effective way to do so.

When the request comes in, instead of launching straight into it, we need to carve ourselves out a little bit of time to do some planning. Think of a project as being like a journey to a destination. The destination is the goal of the project; the plan is the map of how we intend to make the journey.

So we need to figure out the goal (the destination) – and the plan (the map).

The goal
(the destination)

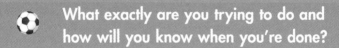

What exactly are you trying to do and how will you know when you're done?

Who's affected by the project and what do they hope to get from it?

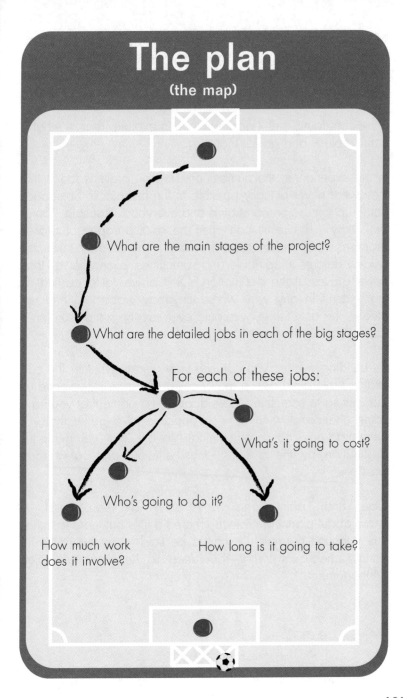

The plan
(the map)

What are the main stages of the project?

What are the detailed jobs in each of the big stages?

For each of these jobs:

What's it going to cost?

Who's going to do it?

How much work does it involve?

How long is it going to take?

Now you'll be able to see quite clearly, if the constraints (whether imposed by somebody else or self-imposed) are achievable or not. If they are, that's great, agree to them and go for it, i.e. execute your plan.

If the constraints aren't achievable then explain/realize what is achievable – and go for that.

In my experience, the number one reason projects fail is that they were never actually possible in the first place. Somebody came up with some constraints and everybody just said, "Sure" or "Okay". The result can often be a catastrophe of broken promises and broken team members. The journey takes the wildest detours imaginable and sometimes, even after all that, never arrives at the destination. Or it arrives at a destination that wasn't in any way where anybody wanted to end up. (Really, the only time you should ever say the word "sure" is if you're buying deodorant!)

By building a plan, you can see very quickly whether the constraints have any basis in reality or not. As a result, you end up committing to something that's doable – a game that you have some chance of winning – as opposed to a game that you never had any chance of winning. Not only that, you get to the destination by the quickest, most efficient and safest route possible.

One final point. This isn't quite all you need to know about planning projects. There's a little but more to it than this – though not much, it has to be said. If you want the full skinny, check out *What You Need To Know About Project Management*.[19]

Do Less – Plan a Project

Take some small request that comes in to you today and plan it as described earlier.

First, figure out the goal/destination – how will you know when the project is over? Who are all the people affected by it? What do they hope to get from it? What would be a good outcome for them?

Then write down the steps in the plan/journey.

Don't cut any corners. Do the plan completely, writing it all down. (Note that this is no big deal. It should only take a matter of minutes to do the plan for a small request.) Then ask yourself whether you found out anything useful by doing this – something you wouldn't have discovered if you had just gone ahead and done the thing.

"If you believe that feeling bad or worrying long enough will change a past or future event, then you are residing on another planet with a different reality system."

[– WAYNE DYER, *Your Erroneous Zones*]

Chapter 7

Don't Feel Guilty

This book is all about a journey to a new and better place in your life – a world of liberation and choice, instead of the world of servitude you may have been enduring. If you've been trying out the "Do Less" challenges, then you've begun that journey. But the journey may not be without its ups and downs. And there are two things, in particular, that might have the potential to seriously derail you. So you need to watch out for them and be ready to deal with them when they appear. These two things are guilt and approval seeking.

1 Guilt

It can come in many different flavours. The one we're talking about here is not what you feel when you've done something bad. Rather it's about recognizing and dealing with that nagging feeling you get when you start to change your behaviour – for example, as you start to apply the concepts of this book.

If you're going to start doing less, you may feel guilty, for example, when everyone around you is still rushing around at warp speed. This could be equally true in work or in your personal life. In work, a particularly common form of guilt is the one when you leave on time having done what you set out to do that day, and other people stay late because that's what the culture of the organization demands. And you can feel guilty all by yourself – you manage to stop just being busy and give yourself a little oasis of time and then you find that "it doesn't feel right"; that you really should be doing something. These are just some examples of the way guilt can come out and bite you.

2 Approval seeking

We all want people to like us. And we would like to feel that when we make some positive improvement in our lives, that those around us would be happy for us and would applaud. In reality that is often not the case. People can disapprove of or resent our new behaviour. Maybe our work colleagues don't like that we're now suddenly leaving on time. (Could well be there's a certain amount of envy at work there too.) Or our partner/wife/husband/housemate may not like that we've cut back on some mundane chore and now invest the time in some more life-enhancing thing. It's a truism that most people are resistant to change and this, in turn, may lead to their disapproving of us and our behaviour.

So what do we do if and when these two things occur? Let's take them in turn.

Guilt and how to avoid it

Guilt – worrying about things that have happened in the past, things that are over and done with, that cannot be changed – has to be one of the silliest and least productive things we do. You would have thought that if you didn't "do" guilt much or at all, then that would be regarded as a good thing. People would compliment you on it, saying things like "My, I like how little you feel guilty about things. How did you get to be like that? Could you teach me to be like that too?"

Nothing, of course, could be further from the truth. If you don't feel guilty, you're regarded as a "bad" person. You don't "care" enough. (Note that this is also true if you're a person who deals well with stress. You're accused of not worrying enough and therefore, not caring enough.)

There also seems to be a tendency to believe that if you feel guilty long enough, then that will somehow eventually expunge your "crime" – that bad thing you did in the past – and you will be exonerated in some sort of way. So let's say you start doing less using the two filters as we've described but then you start to feel guilty. And rather than deal with that guilt, you just carry it around with you, as though – if you do that for long enough – it will somehow make you feel better.

And it has to be said that the idea that you might do less is almost guaranteed to trigger some form of guilt. Doing less brings with it connotations of:

- Being lazy.
- Not being a team player.
- Skiving off.
- Letting other people carry more than their fair share while you carry less than yours.

Here, it's important to distinguish between guilt and learning from your mistakes. Clearly, the latter is a good thing. You analyze what happened and your behaviour. You try to figure out why you did what you did. You then see if there are things you can change or improve and off you go – carrying on with your life, resolving to do better next time out. Build a bridge and get over it, as the saying goes. But endlessly looking back over something that can never be changed? Crazy.

There is another really interesting aspect to guilt that is relevant to us here. Why would we choose to engage in such negative behaviour? What's in it for us? Well, quite a lot actually, as it turns out. Let's say we stay late at the office because we'll feel guilty if we leave on time. Well, that's neat because we can now blame our boss or the culture of the organization or something else for the fact that we are working these long hours and not seeing our children or whatever.

> It's important to distinguish between guilt and learning from your mistakes.

That's great because then all responsibility for dealing with your overloaded situation passes from you. You buy a book like this, read it, do a half-hearted version of what it says and then blame me or the book or somebody or something else for its failure. It certainly wasn't anything to do with you. Psychologists call this a "payoff". You engage in some negative or self-destructive behaviour (in this case, feeling guilty) because you get something positive out of it. The positive you get here is that you can blame somebody else for your situation and not take responsibility for sorting it out yourself.

A question I often ask on my *The Power Of Doing Less* courses is this: "If you're overloaded, who's to blame?" Sometimes people begin with things like, "my boss", "the culture of the organization", "the state of the economy" but pretty soon they all converge on – and agree on – "me!"

If you're overloaded, you're to blame – because you haven't told anybody you're overloaded; because you're not taking any action to deal with the overload. If I'm your boss and I keep throwing stuff over the wall to you and you keep accepting it, then the only conclusion I can draw is that you have the bandwidth to do it. Otherwise you would have told me something different . . . wouldn't you?

Any time you have a guilty moment, write down what exactly it was about, when it occurred, why it occurred and who was involved. Then see what kinds of patterns emerge from this. Are there always certain people involved? Are there certain situations where guilt occurs? Try to understand why these patterns are happening and figure out things you can do to stop them.

For example, maybe the guilt moments always involve your boss. So now, you can start to anticipate these and work on not feeling guilty after an interaction with him/her.

Or the guilt may always be about the same thing. A common one is leaving work on time while other people stay late. Ask yourself whether you felt happier as a result of this behaviour? Did you get to go home and have fun with your kids or a nice evening with your loved one or work on some pet project or hobby of yours?

If you did, isn't that good? And didn't you feel good? And almost certainly didn't you find that, even if you felt guilty some of the time, the rest of the time you "forgot" about your guilt – and just got on with having a nice time. So if you forgot about your guilt once, you can forget about it again. And the more you do this thing that used to make you feel guilty, the more you'll "forget" to feel guilty. Until one day, you'll find yourself not feeling guilty at all and wondering what all the fuss was ever about.

You should be living according to what makes *you* happy, i.e. *your* values, rather than someone else's.

Do Less – Throw Away Your Guilt

For a week or so keep a list of all the times you felt guilty – whether in work or in your life generally. Grade them on a guilt scale of 1 to 10, where 1 is a small amount of guilt and 10 is mind-numbing, depression-causing, sickness-inducing guilt. Now add up the scores.

What did you get? Well, actually, it doesn't matter at all whether they add up to one or a million. It doesn't make the slightest bit of difference. Just throw the list away! Guilt! It belongs in the trash.

GENERATING MYSTIQUE THROUGH DOING LESS

The author J.D. Salinger wrote nothing after 1965 but his reputation was only enhanced by his absence and the mystique it generated. In a rare 1974 interview with *The New York Times*, he explained: "There is a marvelous peace in not publishing . . . I like to write. I love to write. But I write just for myself and my own pleasure." Salinger once referred to publication as "a damned interruption".

An obituary in *The Telegraph* on 28 January 2010 stated, "His career demonstrated that a reputation, even cult status, could be comfortably maintained by a very small amount of published work". (Something for me to ponder there myself!)

Approval-seeking and how to avoid it

We all want people to like us and part of that liking is that we feel that they approve of what we do. If you start to do less, then – as we have seen – that will have a positive impact on you (and on others). But it's as certain as night follows day that not everybody will support or approve of what you're doing.

So what are you to do about that? How are you to feel good about doing less – particularly when other people don't appear to feel good about it? And what's worse, when these are the very same people who may have very much approved of the way you operated previously.

Have a look at the following table.

1904	56	37
1920	60	34
1936	61	37
1964	61	39
1972	61	38
1984	59	41

The figures in the first column are years. The middle column shows the percentages of the popular vote that the winner achieved in the US Presidential election that year. I have chosen these particular years because they are generally regarded as having been "landslide" victories. A landslide victory is one in which a party or a candidate wins by an overwhelming margin, i.e. an overwhelming degree of popularity or approval. Here's the full table.

Year	Winner & percentage	Loser & percentage
1904	Roosevelt 56%	Parker 37%
1920	Harding 60%	Cox 34%
1936	Roosevelt 61%	Landon 37%
1964	Johnson 61%	Goldwater 39%
1972	Nixon 61%	McGovern 38%
1984	Reagan 59%	Mondale 41%

What's striking about these figures is the rightmost column. A landslide victory, "an overwhelming degree of approval", still means that nearly 40% of the people *don't* approve.

> *"In the end it's really only my own approval or disapproval that means anything."*
>
> - AGNETHA FALTSKOG, Ex-Abba singer

What are we to take from this? Well, I think we can safely say that even when some action we take is immensely popular, there will be people who don't approve of it. From which we can pretty much deduce, as Sherlock Holmes might have said, that approval seeking is a mug's game.

So what? We don't want to be liked and approved of? No, of course we want those things. There's no question about that. Recently, I went to see a Bruce Springsteen concert. There were about 35,000 people there. It's probably fair to say that there wasn't one person there who didn't think the Boss was just about the greatest thing that has ever happened. 35,000 people screaming out their approval for you. What must that be like? And not just once, but night after night. Must be an amazing feeling and something that very few of us are ever going to experience.

Most of us probably have more modest expectations. We would like the people around us, the people with whom we come in contact, to like us, to approve of us and the things we do. But is everyone going to approve of us? Don't think so? And even if they did, would they approve of everything we did? Come on now – don't be ridiculous.

Yet sometimes, we feel that we can't move forward or change our behaviour until we get this approval. And that could scupper all of our endeavours. Because we might decide that we *can't* change our behaviour and we daren't start to do less because then that approval we so badly need won't be forthcoming.

When you start to do less, it won't take you long to spot these people and their disapproval. The snide remarks will start coming thick and fast. A fairly classic example is the one where the culture of your organization is the continuous-long-hours culture and you start leaving on time. It won't be long before somebody says to you, "I see you took a half day yesterday". This could equally be true in your domestic life where somebody might start to remark (often unfavourably) on things you've started to do differently. For example, there were some chores you used to do in the morning but now you leave them until some other time because you've started going for a run instead.

The big question is how do you deal with these people? I have two pieces of advice. The first is that you have a policy of zero tolerance. The second is that I've found that the idea of a role model is a good way of tackling this.

Zero tolerance

If you allow people to show their disapproval – they will.

If you don't – they won't.

It's actually as simple as that.

So as soon as you get the first snide remark, deal with it head on. In work, if somebody does try the "I see you took a half day" thing, say, "Yes, I got all the important stuff done and then I went home. I don't deal with unimportant stuff". And if you wanted to, you could add "You should try it sometime". Or – if you're not feeling quite so nasty – "If you like, I'll show you how to do it".

This is all equally true in your personal life. The most obvious examples of when this is likely to occur are when you swap some piece of drudgery for a more life-enhancing thing. Exercise/getting out instead of crashing in front of the TV or messing around on your Facebook page. More fun and less chores. Doing "something" instead of "nothing".

If somebody complains or gets huffy or gives you the silent treatment, explain what you're doing and why. Show them the immense value of getting to live the life you were meant to live – and explain that you could help them to achieve that too.

Role models

And if all of that sounds very in-your-face for you, then this is where role models come in. A role model is somebody we should behave like. Basically you pretend you're somebody else or you ask the question, "What would so-and-so do in these circumstances"? Apart from anything else, it can be fun, imagining that person instead of yourself, at that meeting or confronted with this particular situation or person.

So here are two of my favourites. First is the great American President, Abraham Lincoln, the man who steered the country through four years of terrible civil war, held the Union together and abolished slavery. Here's the man himself:

"If I were to read, much less to answer all the attacks made on me, this shop might as well be closed for any other business. I do the very best I know how – the very best I can; and I mean to keep doing so until the end. If the end brings me out alright, what is said against me won't amount to anything. If the end brings me out wrong, ten angels swearing I was right won't make no difference."[20]

And the other is Winston Churchill. Churchill was the British Prime Minister in 1940. At that time, much of Central and Eastern Europe had been conquered by the seemingly invincible Nazis. France would shortly fall and the Nazis would be in Paris. The US Ambassador in London was briefing Washington on Britain's imminent defeat and surrender. The equally seemingly invincible Japanese Empire was threatening Britain's eastern possessions and the British Army had left most of its equipment behind when it had retreated from Dunkirk. Churchill's own cabinet was wavering and Britain seemed defenceless.

Into this situation stepped Churchill. Talk about cometh the hour, cometh the man. Speaking in the House of Commons on 4 June 1940, Churchill honestly explained the situation and then asked his people to face all this down. Alone, if necessary. You can actually listen to the speech on YouTube – search for "We Shall Fight on the Beaches".

Churchill is also the man who said, "You have enemies? Good. That means that you stood up for something, sometime in your life."

But these are just two of my favourites. Think of your own – people whom you admire, people you think seem to live life on their own terms, who call it as they see it, who never go along with the crowd just to be popular. They don't have to be celebrities or famous people; they could equally be people who are part of your life.

The next time you feel resistance from someone when you're trying to do less, try to picture somebody you really admire there in your shoes and ask yourself the following questions. Would that person you admire have:

■ Changed their position just because of disapproval? For instance, would they have stayed late just because it was the done thing to do?

■ Watered down some statement they wanted to make or altered their position on some issue or not passed on bad news? For example, would they have said that a particular project's constraints were achievable when their planning had told them that they definitely weren't?

■ Felt unhappy because somebody disagreed with them? Would they have become depressed because somebody was sulking or wasn't speaking to them?

■ Gone along with the crowd? Would they have worked all the hours god sent just because everybody else did it?

■ Said "yes" when they should have said "no"? Would they have agreed to a deadline when it was clearly impossible?

■ Been intimidated by anybody – a boss or co-worker or family member or friend who expressed disapproval of their behaviour?

In summary — you have to continue to focus on what matters to you — what your right stuff is. You may well get push back/ resistance from other people. Sadly, that's just the way the world is. It's a bonus if people support you. It's an even bigger bonus if they're interested in learning from you. But however they react, remember that it's your life, not theirs. It only matters that you approve of yourself and your actions. The approval of others is pleasant but irrelevant.

So finally

It may be that when you start to do less, these evil twins of guilt and approval seeking will appear. The first thing is not to be surprised if they do. It probably happens to everybody who goes down this road and who makes the journey we are making.

As I've tried to show, neither of them are very smart things to engage in — and that idea alone may be enough to stop you from even giving them the time of day. Nor are they inevitable parts of our lives and of being a human being. They can and should be expunged, excised, thrown over the side. Don't let other people foist these things on you. Resist when they do. Operate a zero tolerance policy. You'll be making your life and the world generally a better place.

Do Less – Live the Life You Were Meant to Live

Spend a whole day doing less. By this I mean: do what really matters to you – in work and in your personal life – and leave it at that. While you're doing this, if anybody disapproves or you find yourself feeling guilty, deal with it right there and then.

This is a tough one – and you could find yourself feeling quite different at the end of the day. You may feel like you behaved quite "out of character" today. It might almost feel like you had been a different person entirely during the day. That's all good.

Before you go to sleep spend some time writing down what happened, how people reacted, what you did, how you felt then and how you feel now.

"Sow a thought,
and you reap
an act;
Sow an act, and
you reap a habit;
Sow a habit,
and you reap
a character;
Sow a character,
and you reap
a destiny."

[– SAMUEL SMILES, 19th century
Scottish author]

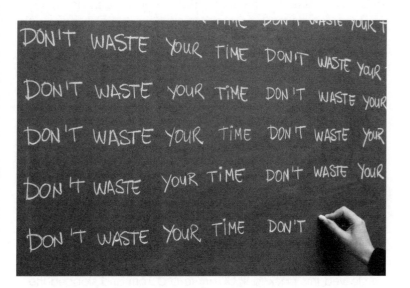

Chapter 8

It's About
Good Habits

If you look on the internet, you'll find lots of articles that begin with the words, "Research has shown it takes twenty one days to form a new habit". If you then go to find out what this research actually is, you'll be sadly disappointed. It appears that there was one study carried out in the 1960s where the author observed that it took 21 days for amputees to adjust to the loss of a limb. Therefore, he concluded, all habits can be changed in 21 days. Hmmm.

More recent research, for example at University College London,[22] shows that it actually takes different people different periods of time to change habits. If you've been doing the "Do Less" challenges so far, then you've already begun to change your habits. In fact, it may be that the change has already taken place. In the online course I teach based on this book, I got an email from one participant saying this:

> "Thank you for this. It has been immensely useful for me to be reminded to respect myself and my precious time. I had let things slip to the point where I was working from 9:00 am until 1:00 am routinely and most weekends. I've been on this treadmill for the past three years. I've now clawed this back to 9:00 am to 6:00 pm and stopped the weekends altogether. Funny how the world didn't end. Thank you for reminding me of what is important!"

And that was three weeks into what is meant to be a ten-week course. There's a changed habit for you!

Most of the "Do Less" challenges in the preceding chapters were about declining things. They showed you that it was okay to decline things. In fact, it wasn't just okay, it was good – very good indeed, in fact, in many situations. The purpose of these challenges was to get you out of the habit of reacting with a "How can I fit this in to an already overcrowded life"?

If you think about it, the habit that I was encouraging you to develop by doing these challenges was that you should react with a "Do I really have to do this?" instead of a "How can I fit this in?"

"Do I really have to do this?" is a good habit and hopefully you're well on the way to developing it or you're already there. But you can improve on that still further. "Do I really have to do this?" is good but it's *reactive*. Something comes in and you decide whether you have to bat it away or not. It's good but it's *defensive*. It carries with it the implication that you already have a full day or a crowded life and you'd rather not make it any fuller or more crowded.

But what if, instead, you became *proactive* and *offensive*? What if, instead of thinking in terms of full days and a crowded life, you thought of empty days and a life waiting to be filled? What if instead of reacting with a "Do I really have to do this?" you reacted with a "Why should I invest my precious time in this?"

This chapter, then, contains an additional bunch of "Do Less" challenges that are about encouraging that mindset and building that habit. Make it your habit and you'll experience the full awesome power of doing less.

Do Less #1 Become More Creative

In a wonderful talk on creativity[23], John Cleese of Monty Python fame explains that "creativity is not a talent. It is a way of operating." He describes five steps necessary to engage in this way of operating. We would recognize the first two of these steps as classic "Do Less" behaviour.

These two steps involve creating what Cleese calls "an oasis of quiet":

1. Find a place where you won't be disturbed.
2. Set aside time – he suggests 90 minutes is a good place to start – in which you are going to not do any of the normal day-to-day things that soak up so much of our time. Instead you are going to create this oasis of time and this is where – hopefully – the creativity will happen.

If you want to know what the other steps are – not to mention hearing some good "how many _____ does it take to change a lightbulb" jokes, you can watch the rest of the talk on YouTube.

Do Less #2 Vegetate (A Bit Anyway)

When that internal couch potato calls, say "Yes, I'm coming". Fridays are my night for this. No cooking, order-in, minimum effort everything. Some nice wine or a couple of beers and food that might be bad for me! Don't ask me to do anything on Friday night. I feel that, mostly, I'm a pretty productive kind of guy and I get lots done, but I turn off the productivity machine on Friday nights. Enough time for that again when the next work day comes round.

Do Less #3 Down Tools

I love Fridays. In the unlikely event that I ever start a religion, its holy day will be Friday. I'll work hard, Monday through Thursday, no problem. I'll even do that on Friday morning. But come Friday afternoon I just want to have fun. In work, I'll down tools on any "proper" work and instead read things I've been meaning to read, or check out some ideas or thoughts I've had. I'll review the week and think about the upcoming week. I'll write in my diary. I'll try to let my head empty and see if any creative thoughts come rushing (or sneaking) in. I'll ask big questions like: how can I be better – in work, in life? I'll try to see things with fresh eyes. Of course, this doesn't have to be on a Friday if you don't want it to be. But pick a day, or an afternoon, to down tools – and do just that.

Do Less #4 Self-Employed? Fair Enough, But Not 100 Hours a Week

If you're self-employed or run a small business (as I do myself), life can be jammed full of work-related trivia. So in order to separate what's wildly important from what isn't, make a list of the wildly important that begins with these three things in this (priority) order:

1   Money – don't run out of it (cash flow).
2   Current customers – give them your all.
3   New customers – find them.

Now explain to me – and more importantly to yourself – why there should be anything else on this list?

Why should I invest my precious time in this? If it isn't one of these three things then you shouldn't!

Do Less #5 – Say "No" When People Delegate Stuff To You

You may feel you're in a job where you can't say "no". But look, you've got to give it a try. You'll find that the world won't stop turning. The sky won't fall, planets won't collide. So here's a way that might work for you. Instead of treating it seriously, make a game out of it.

For instance, for a whole day decline every second request that comes your way. And if a request happens to come from the greatest of all bosses, you can choose to go for it or chicken out. But if you go for it and you succeed, give yourself a prize/reward after work or at the weekend.

Do Less #6 – Get Your Weekends Back

In most countries, the 5 day week/8 hour day only became law during the 20th century. Before that most people worked – in factories or on the land – from dawn until dusk in summer and 10–16 hours a day in winter. And that was seven days a week! The notion that we might have had two consecutive days in a week to ourselves, to do with as we would, was a dream for most of our ancestors.

So weekends are wonderful. They're glorious. And the idea that we would blow our weekends on trivia would appall those people who fought and agitated so hard for the privilege we now enjoy.

So weekends are a time when you do really need to ask, "Why should I invest my precious time in this?"

Look back over the weekend just gone. How much of it was spent on trivia or nothing in particular? And how much on the things that really matter to you? (And please notice I'm making no judgement here about what might be important to you. If spending half of Sunday in bed asleep is what really matters to you, then go for it.)

But if your weekends are going on nothing in particular, it's time to make a change. You can do that in one of three ways:

1   Plan your next weekend to only/mostly contain wildly important stuff; or
2   As your next weekend unfolds and potential things to do present themselves,
     ask "Why should I invest my precious time in this"? If you can't come up with
     a good enough answer, say "Next"; or
3   Plan a completely free weekend – a blank canvas – and just see what comes up
     or takes your fancy. This could turn out to be another really good way of figuring out what really matters to you.

Notice too that all the same comments apply to your evenings after work. This is also a privilege that many of our forbears didn't get to enjoy. And again, no judgement. Some evenings I *will* crash in front of the telly after a tough day. But not *every* evening.

Do Less #7 – Separate Out The "Noise"

For one week, maintain a list of all the things you did in your personal life. I don't mean things like "ate breakfast" or "had a shower" or "slept". Let's assume that you *did* get up, washed, had breakfast, went to work and came home again. But what happened *after* that? (Or indeed before it – if you're an early bird.)

What did you do on each of the five weekdays and the weekend? Record also roughly how much time went into each of the things you did.

At the end of the week, review your list. Against each item, note whether it was "noise" and whether it "mattered"?

Are you happy with what you see? If not, you know what to do.

Do Less #8 – Cut Out The Crap

Make a list of everything you have to do today (or this week) and split it into what's Wildly Important and what Isn't. Rip off the column of what *isn't* wildly important and throw it away.

Do Less #9 – Turn Off The Box

Switch off your laptop/tablet/phone/TV (or anything else that glares you in the eye) at a set time every evening for a week. And stick to it. Whether this allows you more relaxation time, gets you a better night's sleep, or simply gets you focused on something else that needs to be done, notice how much better you'll feel, just from this one little change.

Do Less #10 – Make a List Of The Things You Want To Get Done

Make a list of the things you'd like to do or experience or achieve in your life over the next say, six months or year. When something that might take up your time comes along, ask the question, "Why should I invest my precious time in this?"

If the answer isn't "Because it will progress one of the items on my list", then forget it.

Do Less #11 – Have A Free Day

Aim to have at least one completely free day a week – or, if that's too scary, one evening. That doesn't mean you just have to sit there doing nothing (although you can if you want to of course!). But by having no plan to do *anything*, you might be surprised to see where it takes you.

Do Less #12 – Meditate/Clear Your Head

No, I don't sit in a Lotus position, close my eyes and chant. (I've tried for years, and have done Yoga, but I've never been able to get myself into a Lotus position.) I just walk the dog. Or if she isn't interested I go by myself. For me, it has to be at least half an hour before the ideas start coming but then they come in droves. (They're not all sensible but they're not all stupid either.) I used to run marathons and distance running served the same purpose. So you could find your equivalent. What enables you to quiet your mind and get in touch with your subconscious?

Do Less #13 – Just Do The Things That Really Matter To You

The whole book has been about working out what the right stuff is for you, and cutting out all the other crap. With the rubbish out the way, you should be in a pretty good position to do the right stuff with a clear mind. Even if they're huge, every journey begins with a single step. *"Petit a petit"*, as the French say – little by little. Now it's time to get started!

We've said it numerous times – behaviour change can be difficult. It can be difficult for us and those around us. I've tried to give you a whole menu of things to try. Like a regular menu, you don't need to eat everything on it. Try different things and find what you like – what works for you. If things feel a bit weird or different or out of character, that's okay – it's only to be expected.

The thing to not lose sight of is what these changes are going to do for you. They're going to enable you to live the life you really wanted to live. Nothing short of that.

In his now famous Stanford University commencement speech,[24] Steve Jobs underlined the notion that death is a potent catalyst for life-altering change: "Remembering that I'll be dead soon is the most important tool I've ever encountered to help me make the big choices in life."

We'll all be dead a long time. While we're alive let's make it everything it was meant to be.

"It is impossible you should take true root but by the fair weather that you make yourself; it is needful that you frame the season of your own harvest."

[– WILLIAM SHAKESPEARE, English playwright and poet]

Chapter 9

The **Harvest**

The power of doing less manifests itself in many ways. We talked about liberation in Chapter 3 and that's probably as good a place as any to start.

If you've done the "Do Less" challenges as we've gone along, the monkey is well and truly off your back. You're no longer chained to that great pile of stuff, dragging it around with you, putting vast amounts of time into the vain hope that you'll clear it. You're free of all that now. There's still a pile, of course, but now you pick and choose what you're going to invest your precious time – your precious life – in.

You've got clarity. No longer is the pile a great amorphous mass of stuff. Now you see that some things really matter and lots of stuff is just chickenshit. The stuff that really matters, the big things you plan to do with your life – buying a house, changing career, going on your dream holiday, starting a business, whatever – now draw you to them with magnetic force. All the other stuff . . . well, you now see it as the life destroying crap it really is. Spend a day or an evening or a weekend on the stuff that really matters and even though you may be physically or mentally tired at the end of it, you are energized and uplifted. You have a feeling that things are really starting to happen for you. Conversely, spend time on the trivia and you find yourself depleted. You find yourself trying to figure out ways to avoid it in the future.

You've got focus. Things that you had previously pushed into "next year", because you didn't have the time to plan them properly or the energy to visualize doing them right, are now in focus and start feeling achievable. And part of that focus is that things get done right – whether in work or in your life generally – you have the time to do something properly, instead of putting a band aid over it.

You're less stressed. Now you've got time for everything. And the things you don't get done? Well hey, they don't matter because they never mattered anyway. Without the stress, you can then ditch some of the things that you may have used to cope with the stress. Something like drinking, for example, becomes a pleasure again rather than a crutch. Or anger – that tense, wound-up, ready to explode kind of feeling – will have faded away. In all probability you're feeling healthier as well.

You've got time. There are spaces in your week that are now blank canvases just waiting to be filled.

You've become a productivity machine. Think about this for a moment. Really think about it. Think about the wonderful paradox whereby you're doing *less* but you're *more* productive. You're achieving more. Getting more done. Living much more the life you wanted to live.

And you're not a hyperactive productivity machine. It's still okay – and you have the time – to switch the productivity machine off, to do nothing. To reflect, to sit and just be, to enjoy the moment, to be creative, to see opportunities that you would certainly have missed when you were running around like a blue-arsed fly.

In short – you're happier. Much happier.

And the wonderful – the really, extraordinary, remarkable, really quite unbelievable, beautiful thing – is that you didn't have to do new or more or extra things.

In fact, you did the exact opposite.

As soon as you stop doing, the power of doing less starts to flow.

Take **better** care
of your body

Learn a
language

LEARN
A
MUSICAL
INSTRUMENT

TAKE UP A **NEW** SPORT

Take
a
trip

START A
NEW
HOBBY

Become **involved** in a charity

BREAK OUT **AND**
COLLABORATE
ON A COMMUNITY
OR ONLINE PROJECT

Start a **business**

Be spontaneous

Find a
course
to **attend**

Check out
great
speakers online

TALK TO **ABSOLUTELY EVERYBODY**
YOU MEET — MAKE A **CONNECTION**

Talk to
people
you might
learn from

Go on a
nature hike

Dance in
the rain

PLANT
SOMETHING
EDIBLE

TRY AND CREATE
YOUR **OWN** RECIPE

Do
a big activity
for charity

LEARN
TO
JUGGLE

Connect **with someone** new

WAKE UP **AN**
EARLY HOUR

Make a **gift**
for someone

Overcome a fear

Spend
time
outdoors

Become **a**
mentor

Donate **blood**

Give
someone
a compliment

Do **good**

References

1 *American Time Use Survey Summary* http://www.bls.gov/news. release/atus.nr0.htm.

2 http://www.huffingtonpost.com/2012/05/24/11-countries-with-the-longest-working-hours_n_1543145.html#slide= 1018059.

3 Holland, James, *Dam Busters: The Race To Smash The Dams 1943*, London: Transworld, 2012.

4 DeMarco, Tom. *The Deadline: A Novel About Project Management*, New York: Dorset House, 1997.

5 Allen, David, *Getting Things Done: How to Achieve Stress-free Productivity*, London: Piatkus, 2002.

6 Bar-Eli, M., Azar, O.H., Ritov, I. & Keidar-Levin, Y. (2007). Action bias among elite soccer goalkeepers: The case of penalty kicks. *Journal of Economic Psychology*, 28, 606–21.

7 http://blogs.hbr.org/cs/2012/01/five_myths_of_a_ceos_first_100.html.

8 Taylor, A J P, *War By Time-Table: How the First World War Began*, London: Macdonald, 1969.

9 http://www.amazon.com/Band-Brothers-Blu-ray-Scott-Grimes/dp/B0006TSSNG/ref=sr_1_2?s=books&ie=UTF8&qid=13605 95596&sr=1-2&keywords=band+of+brothers+dvd.

10 Ambrose, Stephen E., *Band of Brothers: E Company, 506th Regiment, 101st Airborne from Normandy to Hitler's Eagle's Nest*, New York: Simon & Schuster, 2001.

11 Fussell, Paul, *Wartime: Understanding and Behavior in the Second World War*, Oxford: Oxford University Press, 1990.

12 Cleese, John & Booth, Connie, *The Complete Fawlty Towers*, London: Methuen, 2000.

13 Attwood, Janet Bray & Chris, *The Passion Test: The Effortless Path to Discovering Your Destiny*, London: Simon & Schuster, 2006.

14 Bannatyne, Duncan, *Wake Up and Change Your Life*, London: Orion, 2009.

15 Bolles, Richard N, *What Colour Is Your Parachute? 2013: A Practical Manual for Job-Hunters and Career-Changers*, New York: Ten Speed Press, 2012.

16 Robbins, Anthony, *Awaken the Giant Within: How to Take Immediate Control of Your Mental, Emotional, Physical and Financial Destiny!*, New York: Free Press, 1992.

17 Daniel Day-Lewis on acting http://www.bbc.co.uk/news/entertainment-arts-21227022.

18 Covey, Steven, *The 7 Habits of Highly Effective People*, New York: Simon & Schuster, 2004.

19 O'Connell, Fergus, *What You Need To Know About Project Management*, Chichester: Capstone Publishing Ltd, 2011.

20 Carpenter, Francis B., *Six Months at the White House*, Forgotten Books, 2012.

21 Winston S Churchill – We Shall Fight on the Beaches http://www.youtube.com/watch?v=MkTw3_PmKtc&feature=fvwrel.

22 University College London Health Behaviour Research Centre http://www.ucl.ac.uk/hbrc/diet/lallyp.html.

23 John Cleese on creativity http://www.youtube.com/watch?v=f9rtmxJrKwc.

24 Steve Jobs Stanford commencement address 2005 http://www.youtube.com/watch?v=VHWUCX6osgM.

Image Credits

Pviii Head in the sand – © thorbjorn66/istockphoto.com

Px All around Asia you will find bicycles overloaded with too much cargo and just simple baskets – TheCrazyTravel/Shutterstock.com

Pxii Man Weighed Down by Credit Card Debt – © MHJ/istockphoto.com

Pxii The Earth with City Skyline and Planes – © MHJ/istockphoto.com

Pxiii Man floating with a Big Red Balloon – © MHJ/istockphoto.com

Pxiv Many gold fish together as symbol of teamwork – Sergey Nivens/Shutterstock.com

Pxix Let it go, a message in the sand – Perspectives – Jeff Smith/Shutterstock.com

P1 Complacency – © biffspandex /istockphoto.com

P2, 31, 33, 47, 49, 50, 59, 70, 76, 84, 85, 86, 92 and 111 Abstract paper with sunburst – Petrov Stanislav/Shutterstock.com

P6 World War Two – US Air Force Background – © KeithBishop / istockphoto.com

P13 Yellow post it notes with various written to-do tasks affixed to the corkboard – pryzmat/Shutterstock.com

P17, 18, 27, 28 Graph showing growth progress made from orange bricks – Zelfit/Shutterstock.com

P25 Wasting water leaks into overfilled glass photo – Forster Forest/Shutterstock.com

P37 Funnel presentation template with space for different elements – Janos Levente/Shutterstock.com

P41 Finding The Right Key – © JerryPDX/istockphoto.com

P55 Merry-go-round twisting fast in the night with thousands lights – Maksim Toome/Shutterstock.com

P63 Gorilla Thinking – James Laurie/Shutterstock.com

P65 Set of office accessories isolated on a white background – Triff/Shutterstock.com

P66 Square Tick/Cross badge set – © simmosimosa/istockphoto.com

P71 Vector clipboard – Alhovik/Shutterstock.com

P75 Sheet of paper for notes and paper clip – sergign/Shutterstock.com

P87 Child saying no – Velazquez77/Shutterstock.com

P89 A young gal at the bowling alley – playing 'crazy bowl' – planet5D LLC/Shutterstock.com

P91 A goldfish going off with his own ideas – plampy/Shutterstock.com

P96–97 Drawing on the frying pan with a white background – Yusuf YILMAZ/Shutterstock.com

P100 Football Stadium – © piart/istockphoto.com

P101 Soccer game plan – © oleganus/istockphoto.com

P105 A box of holiday chocolates lays open on a table . . . there is only one piece left – Thomas M Perkins/Shutterstock.com

P121 Wasting time – © aluxum/istockphoto.com

P133 Silhouette of girl and dove, freedom and peace abstract concept background – Pan Xunbin/Shutterstock.com

P147 Stacks of Books – © filo/istockphoto.com

Acknowledgements

Big thank you, first of all, to Dermott Bolger, Eamonn Toland and John Sheridan for their contributions.

As always, thank you to my redoubtable and tireless agent, Darin Jewell.

I'm grateful to all of the team at Wiley – Vicky Kinsman, Grace O'Byrne, Megan Saker, Ashley Mackie, Louise Campbell, Laura Cooksley, Iain Campbell – but especially to the wonderful Jonathan Shipley and Jenny Ng. Their support, help, creativity, suggestions, pushing me to up my game and ferociously hard work made all the difference.

About the Author

The Sunday Business Post has described **Fergus O'Connell** as having "more strings to his bow than a Stradivarius". Fergus is one of the world's leading authorities on project management. His company – ETP (www.etpint.com) – and his project management method – The Ten Steps – have influenced a generation of project managers.

In 2003 this method was used to plan and execute the Special Olympics World Games, the world's biggest sporting event that year. Fergus's experience covers projects around the world; he has taught project management in Europe, North America, South America and Asia. He has written on the subject for many publications including *The Wall Street Journal*. He has lectured at University College Cork, Trinity College Dublin, Bentley College, Boston University, the Michael Smurfit Graduate School of Business and on television for the National Technological University. He holds two patents.

Fergus is the author of 13 business books. The first of these, *How to Run Successful Projects – the Silver Bullet*, has become both a bestseller and a classic and has been constantly in print for over 20 years. His book on common sense entitled *Simply Brilliant* – also a bestseller and now in its fourth edition – was runner-up in the W H Smith Book Awards 2002. His books have been translated into 20 languages.

He has two children and now lives in Ireland.

You can contact Fergus at Fergus.oconnell@etpint.com about his books, or for consultancy, training or speaking work. You can also visit his Facebook page at http://www.facebook.com/fergusoconnell.

www.fergusoconnell.com

ALSO BY FERGUS O'CONNELL

Non-fiction

HOW TO RUN SUCCESSFUL PROJECTS – THE SILVER BULLET, 3RD EDITION

HOW TO RUN SUCCESSFUL HIGH-TECH PROJECT-BASED ORGANIZATIONS

HOW TO RUN SUCCESSFUL PROJECTS IN WEB-TIME

SIMPLY BRILLIANT – THE COMPETITIVE ADVANTAGE OF COMMON SENSE, 3RD EDITION

HOW TO DO A GREAT JOB – AND GO HOME ON TIME

FAST PROJECTS: PROJECT MANAGEMENT WHEN TIME IS SHORT

HOW TO GET MORE DONE: SEVEN DAYS TO ACHIEVING MORE

WORK LESS, ACHIEVE MORE: GREAT IDEAS TO GET YOUR LIFE BACK

EARN MORE, STRESS LESS: HOW TO ATTRACT WEALTH USING THE SECRET SCIENCE OF GETTING RICH

WHAT YOU NEED TO KNOW ABOUT PROJECT MANAGEMENT

ZERO WASTE IN BUSINESS

Fiction

CALL THE SWALLOW

THE FOUR LIGHTS QUARTET:

1   STARLIGHT

2   THE PHOTOGRAPHS OF GETTYSBURG: SUNLIGHT

3   MOONLIGHT (AUTUMN 2013)

4   CANDLELIGHT (SPRING 2014)

BOOKS FOR CHILDREN

HOW TO PUT A MAN ON THE MOON IF YOU'RE A KID

147

"I will arise
and go
now, and go
to Innisfree."